THE ESSENTIAL GUIDE TO
Coffee
THE ESSENTIAL BEAN

Coffee

THE ESSENTIAL GUIDE TO THE ESSENTIAL BEAN

Catherine Calvert
Recipes by Jane Stacey

HEARST BOOKS
NEW YORK

Library of Congress Cataloging-in-Publication Data

Coffee : the essential guide to the essential bean.
p.   cm.
ISBN 0-688-13328-2

1. Cookery (Coffee) 2. Coffee brewing.   3. Coffee
TX819.C6.C64 1994
641.6'373--dc20   94-8503
                                                            CIP

Printed in Italy

First Edition

1   2   3   4   5   6   7   8   9   1 0

Produced by Smallwood and Stewart, Inc., New York City

Book design by Susi Oberhelman
Illustrations by Ed Lam
Edited by Evie Righter

Contents

· ·

Introduction

. . . .

CUP YOUR HANDS AROUND A STEAMING mug of coffee and you have history in your grasp; one sip of the fragrant brew, and you've joined the long line of humanity that has found joy in the bright red berry that grows on the coffee tree. As with any substance deemed valuable, coffee has a history full of wars and romances, its origins lost in legend, and its satisfactions an alchemy greater than simply the mixing of roasted beans and boiling water. Through its history, coffee has made pirates of grandees, and poets of mere mortals. "A cup of coffee—real coffee—home browned, home ground, home made, that comes to you dark as a hazel eye, but changes to a golden bronze as you temper it with cream that never cheated...such a cup of coffee is a match for twenty blue devils and will exorcise them all," wrote the American philosopher Henry Ward Beecher.

Originally coffee wasn't a beverage at all. It was goat fodder, if you believe the legend of Kaldi the Abyssinian herdsman. It is said that more than a thousand years ago, this young goatherd came upon his flock cavorting around a bush and feeding upon its bright red berries. Inspired by their transports, Kaldi tried some berries himself, and joined in the romp. A monk passing on his way to daily prayers was struck by what he saw and took some berries for himself. Later, when he mixed them with water and drank the fragrant concoction, he found that he could pray all night with remarkable clarity. This new aid to spirituality soon spread throughout monasteries in Arabia.

In Middle Eastern society, coffee has always been an essential medium of social exchange. In this eighteenth-century print, a servant pours a small cup of rich, dark Turkish brew from an ibrik.

Historians trace coffee's origins to Ethiopia, where it still grows wild in the rainforest. From very early times, warriors going off to battle or travelers on journeys would wrap beans in animal fat to help fight fatigue. The Ethiopians who conquered and ruled Yemen probably introduced the bean

to the Arab world, where its medicinal qualities were prized as well; doctors prescribed it as an aid to feeling good. Dervishes whirled faster, scholars and artists could work all night

By the sixteenth century, the principle of roasting beans and adding them to boiling water to make

a beverage was established in Arabia, and the preparation of coffee became a secular ceremony; the first coffeehouses, called *qahveh khaneh,* were established in Mecca for those who liked to sip, talk, and listen to music. As wine was forbidden to Moslems and water was scarce, coffee became central to a man's day—and a woman's too: One of the few grounds on which a woman could divorce was a man's refusal to provide her with coffee.

Coffee's arrival in Europe is not well documented. Certainly Venetian traders who traversed the world would have encountered the Arabs' coffee, which was part of any merchant's bargaining ritual. When Venetians began to brew their own around 1615, some feared its allure, and called it the "bitter invention of Satan." It took Pope Clement VIII (1536-1605) to try a cup and give it

In the eighteenth century, coffee became the drink of European aristocracy, and elaborate ceremonies grew up around its preparation and serving.

In the Colonies, establishments such as The Old London Coffeehouse in Philadelphia followed the same tradition as those in Europe as places to meet friends, argue politics, perhaps brew up a revolution.

his blessing before the beverage was generally accepted. Once again, it was thought so potent that its medicinal benefits were celebrated before it became the sociable drink it was to be.

The Arabs who cultivated the coffee plant wanted to safeguard it from enterprising European traders, and for years they banned visitors from plantations and made certain only sterile plant stock was exported. But legend has it that in the mid-eighteenth century a Moslem pilgrim from India managed to smuggle out seven seeds and planted them at home, where they flourished. The Dutch also carried off seeds from India to Java, filling their trading ships bound for Europe. Their great mistake, however, was in attempting to flatter Louis XIV (1638-1715) of France by presenting him with a coffee tree, carried with great care from Java. The tree lived undisturbed until 1723, when Gabriel Mathieu de Clieu, an enterprising French naval officer serving in Martinique, realized that the island's climate resembled that of Java, and that the royal coffee tree might thrive there. Making off with a seedling, he tended it day and night on the voyage home to Martinique, even sharing his slim water ration with the little bush. It arrived green and thriving (he a bit the worse for wear). After planting the seedling and surrounding it with thorn bushes and guards, he eventually made his fortune helping to create the coffee plantations that soon appeared throughout the West Indies.

More skullduggery led to the introduction of coffee in Brazil. In 1727, Brazil sent the charming and handsome lieutenant colonel Francisco de Melo Palheta, an excellent surveyor, to mediate a boundary dispute between two coffee-growing colonies, Dutch and French Guiana. Mornings, he measured the territory; evenings, he took the measure of the French governor's wife. At his farewell banquet, she pressed a pretty bouquet upon him in which were hidden coffee seedlings, the roots of today's enormous Brazilian coffee industry.

From its original uses in medicine and religion, coffee began to take its place on tables around the world. The brew from a bean that had caused skullduggery, sedition, and supersition, now gained stylish acceptance. These days it is the world's most universal beverage, and a broad belt of coffee plantations circles the globe, coinciding with the particular conditions of heat, moisture, soil, and altitude that the plant needs to thrive. Many of the most ancient methods of cultivation and harvesting this extraordinarily valuable cash crop remain.

Countries that love coffee have spent the centuries since its introduction refining their appetite for the bean, seeking distinctive flavors that reflect their own culture's tastes for sweetness or bitterness, and reserving particular times each day for their enjoyment of the drink. The Frenchman who dunks his croissant in a steaming cup of *café au lait*, the Italian who tosses back his small cup of espresso several times a

Fine wood paneling, luxurious velvet upholstery, elegant patrons, a cup of coffee—this Viennese scene is almost timeless.

day, the American who loves his java in a heavy white mug at the diner or in an elegant cup in a sleek coffee bar are part of the long line of men and women who have discovered the flavor, the fragrance, the comfort to be found in the ceremonies of coffee.

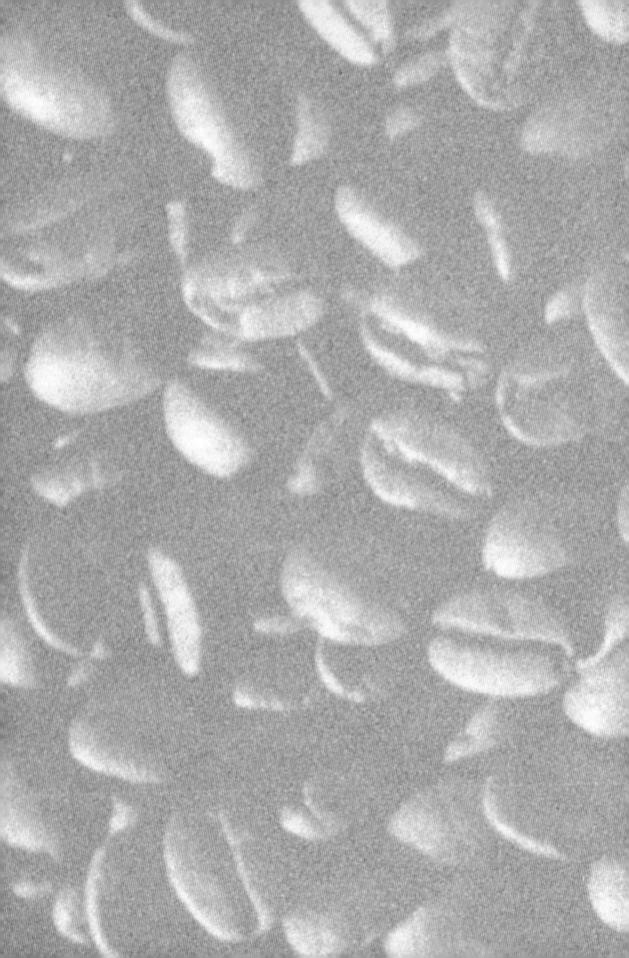

1

European Traditions

In Europe the most obstreperous

nations are those most addicted

to coffee. We rightly speak of a

storm in a teacup as the tiniest

disturbance in the world, but out

of a coffee-cup come hurricanes.

—ROBERT LYND

European Traditions

. . . .

AS THE DRINKING OF COFFEE BECAME
more and more popular, countries formed their own rituals
around the beverage reflecting their individual national character,
their appetite for ease and entertainment, their energies and their
commerce. Traders introduced the drink; it remained for hostesses
and men about town to pour the pot. The coffee cultures of
central Europe, Italy, France, and Central America have such
long-established customs that they form part of our very vision of
a country and its people—who could imagine Paris without
thinking of its cafés, or Italy without the aroma of espresso? In
every case, coffee, as both the centerpiece of sociability and a
cherished private ritual, is true to its Middle Eastern roots.

Each region's taste for coffee is a sum of its history, its work
habits, its love of leisure, its style—and even the local weather.
(The Dutch in their gray-skied country say,
"Coffee has two virtues: It is wet and warm.")
Scandinavians, with their long cold winters, are
the major imbibers of coffee in the world,
followed closely by Holland, Belgium, and
Austria. Americans consume less—about a third
of that drunk by the Scandinavians—though,
suprisingly, they drink more than the Italians.
The English cling to their teapots.

*The coffeehouses
of central Europe have
always been bastions
of imperial formality,
complete with starched
white tablecloths and
gleaming silver trays.*

Central Europe

Germany and the remnants of the Austro-Hungarian Empire share a rich coffee heritage; there are coffeehouses grand and simple scattered throughout the region. It was a German botanist and physician who in 1582 wrote the first western description of the Arabs' beverage: "Very good drink they call Chaube that is almost as black as ink and very good in illness, especially of the stomach." About a hundred years later, and not too far removed, the Austrians were experiencing a less pleasant introduction to coffee: In 1683 the Turks conquered and occupied the city of Vienna. Eventually the Turks were routed, and triumphant Austrian nobles sorted through the spoils left behind. Gold and supplies were quickly spoken for, but no one wanted the sacks of little beans—except Franz George Kolschitzky, an adventurer who had lived among the Turks and knew the coffee bean's value. Cleverly, he set men selling coffee in the streets of Vienna, then opened the first coffeehouse, The Blue Bottle.

Kolschitzky's entrepreneurial energy established the reign of coffee in Vienna forever, especially when accompanied by *Kipfel*, those crescent-shaped pastries that reminded the Austrians of the flag of the vanquished Turks. Cream-filled pastries, sugared cakes, *Torten*, strudel, and *Krapfen* (Vienna's famous jam doughnuts) continue to serve as perfect enchancements to mid-European coffee drinking. In Vienna, there are said to be twenty-eight ways of drinking coffee, defined by the type of preparation, size of cup, quantity of cream, or whether it is accompanied by whiskey. The more familiar drinks include *Türkischer* (Turkish coffee) and *Kapuziner* (with whipped cream).

*F*ounded in 1858, the Vörösmarty, like dozens of other Budapest coffeehouses, has endured wars, revolution, socialism, and now capitalism.

The coffeehouses in middle Europe were at their glittering peak around 1900, and some of the best preserved retain their old glamour as well as a firm place in their cities' hearts. Generation after generation has spent hours spooning *schlag* (cream)

Café Mozart

into a cup and suffering the exquisite hesitation of choosing just which slice of *torte* will best complement the moment. A newspaper or magazine is as fit a companion as a good friend settling in for a gossip, and the day passes marked by the glasses of cold water set beside the coffee cup by the waiter.

Though there are many fewer coffeehouses in Vienna than in decades past, and fewer people who allow themselves the luxury of a long afternoon with cream and cakes and coffee, a new generation of young people is discovering such pleasures as Museum, still sparkling with its 1899 fittings of brass and glass and mirrors, or the handsome Landtmann, near the university, once the favorite of Sigmund Freud and now the haunt of journalists, actors, and politicians.

The golden era of Budapest's coffeehouses lasted well into the 1940s and is now undergoing a revival as the city rediscovers its old elegances. Hungarians claim they were drinking coffee a hundred years before the Viennese and Parisians; in 1900 there were six hundred coffeehouses in Budapest. While the aristocracy and the leisure class sought out the cafés trimmed in mirrors and fine draperies, actors, writers, artists, and journalists found a warm reception—and a warm place to work—in a café like the New-York, where a cup of coffee could be stretched for hours while perusing the newspapers held by bamboo sticks. Visitors still seek the New-York out for its art nouveau interiors.

*D*emel in Vienna (preceding page) has served kings and connoisseurs of the pastrymaker's art for more than two hundred years. The selection of exquisite cakes and tortes— now known as a Viennese table— astonishes. (Above and right): As these signs in Vienna and Salzburg proclaim, music and coffee form a fine harmony in cafés all over Austria.

In Germany, the tension between politics and the public's love of coffee color its history. Frederick the Great, irritated at the money flowing into the coffers of foreign coffee merchants, urged his people to abandon their allegiance to the brew for their old favorite, beer. But to no avail—Bach went on to compose the *Coffee Cantata*, after all.

The customs of the last century are still honored. The *Konditoreien* (pastry shops) are wonderful places to choose an *obst torte* (fruit tart) or a slice of chocolate cake and a cup of medium-roast coffee. The handsomest cafés date from the turn of the century, like Das Cafehaus, still standing on the Kurfürstendamm, Berlin's once elegant promenade, while Munich residents can drink coffee in Cafe HAG, founded in 1825 as the court confectioner's establishment. The *kaffeeklatsch* remains the traditional accompaniment to cakes and cups. And gatherings of family and friends continue to revolve around the coffee table.

France

"To write the history of our cafés would almost amount to writing a history of France," said one French historian. Indeed, what could be more identified with France than these cafés, shutters cranked open with the sun as waiters pull spindly-legged tables close together on the sidewalk and the first customers settle in to watch the passing parade, or hold hands and watch each other, or bury themselves in *Le Figaro*. More than twelve thousand cafés enliven the streets of Paris alone. From the beginning, coffee drinking in France had to do with *chic*. A seventeenth-

CAFE Mozart BEI DER OPER

century Turkish ambassador served the fashionable coffee in elegant little cups with gold-fringed napkins amid an atmosphere of luxurious exoticism, and coffee became the rage. In 1686, an Italian named Procopio dei Coltelli opened Café de Procope, the first real Parisian café, which still exists today, though as a restaurant. It was here that artists and intellectuals gathered and Voltaire drank his daily forty cups of coffee mixed with chocolate.

After France's more than three hundred years of experience with the bean, it is no surprise that important moments of the day revolve around it. Talleyrand had his own prescription: "A cup of coffee detracts nothing from your intellect; on the contrary, your stomach is freed by it and no longer distresses your brain; it will not hamper your mind with troubles but give freedom to its working . . . work becomes easier and you will sit down without distress to our principal repast which will restore your body and afford you a calm delicious night." And Flaubert counseled, "Take it without sugar—very swank." Swank coffee remains, in and out of the café. At home, who could begin the morning without a *café au lait*, the milk turning the coffee pale brown, served in a cup big enough to require both hands around it. With a croissant and jam, this is breakfast at its French best.

Surely Parisians are as busy at their jobs as anyone else in the world, but their cafés seemed filled at almost any hour of the day. Waiters are tolerant of those who dawdle all afternoon. "I was often alone, but never lonely," wrote American journalist A. J. Liebling of his time in Paris, much of it spent in a café. Hemingway sought out Aux Deux Magots, where Sartre sipped and smoked and wrote; sitting on one of its red banquettes surrounded by mirrors, you can follow suit, or simply contemplate the fashionables who go there now. Or cross to Café de Flore, with its art deco interior, where Picasso watched the shabby and the chic parade along the streets of the Left Bank.

This Paris café, with the Arc de Triomphe as a backdrop and an elegant boulevard sweeping by its front door, makes it clear why leisurely sipping demi-tasse outdoors is an essential part of life in Paris.

Espresso, in fact, is a French invention. In the early part of the nineteenth century, a machine was developed that boiled water in a tank, and then captured the steam to force the hot water through the coffee. Now the taste is for a *café noir* or *café exprès,* plain black espresso, or *café serré*, made extra strong with half the usual water. *Café allongé* is accompanied by a pitcher of hot water to thin it, and *café au lait* or *café crème* comes with lightly steamed milk. *Café filtre* is filtered coffee, American style.

The French understand that some foods seem made to be eaten with coffee, the marriage bringing out the nuances of both.

After dinner, small rich chocolates are passed with the coffee. And who could resist, in a blue Paris twilight, a cup of coffee served with a delicious Calvados or a marc?

Italy

Italy's coffee traditions, among the most venerable, are thoroughly intertwined with the business and the pleasures of daily life. Yet Italian consumption of coffee remains below that of most of Europe, perhaps because it takes only a small cup of well-prepared espresso to satisfy.

If the French invented the espresso machine, the Italians perfected it and made the fragrant, rich brew their own, to be savored in endless combinations of steamed milk (cappuccino) or alone with a glass of Sambuca. What had been a fairly ornate machine that made coffee to order with a dramatic hiss was streamlined and modernized after World War II by the Gaggia family, producing a machine that forced water through coffee with nine times as much pressure as had been previously possible.

Except for the caffès that spread their tables across the broad piazzas and beneath the arches of a town's center, most coffee is taken standing up at a coffee bar where the espresso machine trickles out each order ("espresso"

Italians make their stand at the bar-caffès throughout Italy, darting in for an espresso pronto, sometimes with a glass of one of the many exotic and colorful Italian bitters and liqueurs.

means by express command) to those who rest an elbow on the marble counter. The regulars order a *basso* (strong) or *doppio* (double). The espresso maker packs a small metal strainer with a favorite finely ground blend that is predominantly made up of the rougher robusta beans—beans roasted for use in espresso remain in the heat so long that the flavor of the more subtle beans would be lost. When pressurized steam from the *macchina a vapore* passes through the coffee grounds, soluble parts of the bean are washed into the cup along with emulsified oils that heighten the coffee's flavor and aroma. A practiced and energetic *barista* is able to serve each order in about a minute, with a blend and flavor that has been tuned to local tastes.

The bar-caffè is the chief dispenser of coffee throughout the day, with natives preferring a particular place for its way with *caffè shakerato*, for instance (shaken with milk and ice) or the assortment of *panini* (small filled rolls picked up for a quick snack). Early-morning drinkers might choose a roll or some *bomboloni* (doughnut-like pastries that are jam- or cream-filled). This informal caffè often serves as the town's center, the place to make a phone call, buy *gelato*, smoke cigarettes; after lunch, a back room may hold most of the men of the neighborhood, nursing their espressos, playing billiards or cards. The menu might include *caffè corretto*, boosted with liqueur; *caffè freddo*, iced in the summer; *caffè macchiato*, "stained" with a drop of milk.

There are regional variations, like Rome's *caffè al vetro*—in a glass—or *caffè valdostano*, a mix of hot coffee, wine, spices, and grappa (a strong liqueur) traditionally served in winter in the Val d'Aosta. Cappuccino and *caffè latte* are reserved for the morning, never for the end of a meal, when a strong black coffee might be accompanied by a *digestivo*, or an interesting grappa.

Venice, the city that early on established a fondness for the coffee its traders brought back

Patrons at Caffè Florian in Venice's Piazza San Marco drink in the beauty of the city and the music of Vivaldi played by a small orchestra (preceding page). Inside, they sip coffee in frescoed rooms, where soft-glowing light falls on gently polished wood (opposite).

from their travels, has been home to the handsome Caffè Florian for centuries. Since 1720 it has stood in the Piazza San Marco, welcoming locals and tourists alike to its frescoed rooms, where the ghosts of former patrons—Goethe, Dickens, Proust, to name a few illustrious ones—hover in the shadows. Other major cities are home to similar long-loved establishments where fair weather brings everyone outside to linger over coffee and conversation. In Rome it's Caffè Greco and L'Aragno; in Florence, the Paszkowski; in Milan, fashionable Cova and art deco Taveggia; in Naples— considered by some the very center of flavorful coffee making thanks to its pure water, fine roasts, and the innate Neapolitan flair for finding the best of life—it's nearly every caffè.

England

If the world is divided into tea drinkers and coffee drinkers, we know where the British heart lies. But in fact coffee has played an important part in English history.

It was from England that the foundations for our own use of coffee were laid. The earliest reference to coffee in England comes in 1637 when a Turkish entrepreneur opened a coffee-house in Oxford. (Signs featuring the word "Turkish" have remained a signature for coffee vending ever since, with turbaned figures on coffee labels or café signs, and fine hotels costuming their coffee servers in pantaloons.) That first Oxford coffeehouse attracted university students—another tradition that sees little sign of waning. Here debate was heated by the potful, and opinions of all sorts had their airing.

By 1652 the first London coffeehouse had opened, its pro-prietor a foreigner, probably from Greece. Here was the true wit's end, where the likes of Samuel Johnson could sit at a table for hours with like-minded souls, telling stories, spinning theories, gossiping energetically. Each house catered to a distinctive clientele; political parties had their particular refuge, every profession its haunt. Lloyd's, the insurance brokers, began as a coffeehouse of the same name, and the great clubs that line Pall Mall today, such as White's, also started as coffeehouses.

That the age of the coffeehouse coincided with the Age of Reason may be no coincidence. In Britain, France, Constantinople, and elsewhere, rulers remained convinced that coffeehouses brewed up sedition as well as coffee. Charles II feared rebellion and closed down English establishments in 1675, but public outcry soon had the doors open again.

Today, countries like Kenya, which produce fine coffee, are, of course, no longer colonies of the British Empire. And because of the vigorous efforts of the British East India Company, the main pot on the English table is tea, not coffee. But "elevenses" at mid-morning remain an important part of the day, when coffee provides a needed break and a warming lift with a plain coffee biscuit. And after fine food, whether in a fine restaurant or at a dinner party at home, well-brewed coffee follows the port, the cigars, and mints covered in bitter chocolate.

LYONS' FRENCH COFFEE

LYONS' FRENCH COFFEE 5d

A BLEND of the FINEST COFFEE and CHICORY ½ LB. NET

The Perfect Flavour

Despite its history as a tea-drinking country, England has its own coffee culture. The Lyons cornerhouse chain had its heyday in the 1930s and contributed to the popularization of coffee in England.

2

America's Cup

Among the numerous luxuries of the table,

unknown to our forefathers, coffee may be

considered as one of the most valuable. It excites

cheerfulness without intoxication; and the

pleasing flow of spirits which it occasions…is never

followed by sadness, languour or debility.

—BENJAMIN THOMPSON

America's Cup

· ·

WHEN THE EIGHTEENTH-CENTURY AMERICAN inventor Benjamin Thompson wrote his praise of coffee, he was not completely accurate. Forefathers and -mothers in America knew coffee very well, whether they were seventeenth-century Dutch settlers who had brought over their own prized coffee cannisters or imported their beans from Dutch colonies such as Java, or eighteenth-century English immigrants who were familiar with the pleasures of the coffeehouse.

In the early days, New York, a rambunctious port city where people of many cultures ebbed and flowed, may have been the place where the beverage was first and most firmly established. Puritans in New England did not encourage a beverage taken in an atmosphere of conviviality, argument, and idleness, and those Frenchified coffee drinkers of New Orleans were far away. The New Amsterdam Dutch loved the chocolate, tea, and coffee that flowed in on their trading fleet, but it took the English and their capture of the city in the 1670s to replace the flagon of beer on the breakfast table with a pot of coffee. Being good New Yorkers, they managed to make money with their choice; William Penn complained about having to pay $4.65 for a pound

In roadside diners across the United States, a cup of java with every meal still reigns supreme. This high-flying example of 1950s architecture displays some of the exuberant iconography spawned by American coffee shops.

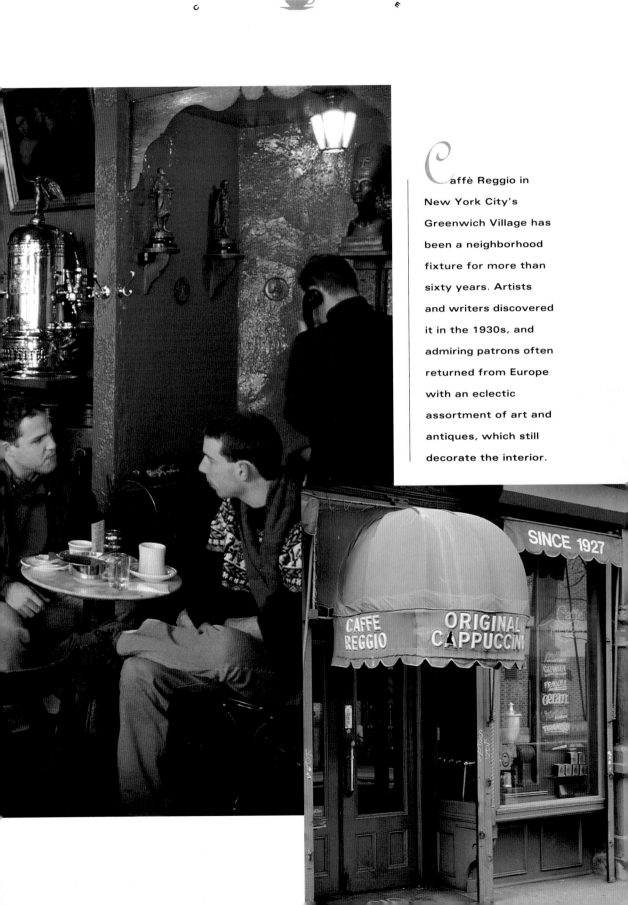

Caffè Reggio in New York City's Greenwich Village has been a neighborhood fixture for more than sixty years. Artists and writers discovered it in the 1930s, and admiring patrons often returned from Europe with an eclectic assortment of art and antiques, which still decorate the interior.

places where a cup of well-made coffee was the centerpiece of a simple menu. Working men turned these cafés into informal clubs, often gathering with friends from their own region in Italy.

Later, artists and writers, and others living on a shoestring made the coffeehouses their own. In San Francisco in the 1950s, cafés like Caffè Trieste and Malvina Caffè attracted the Beats— Jack Kerouac when he wasn't on the road, Lawrence Ferlinghetti when he wasn't in the City Lights bookshop. The Figaro and Caffè Reggio in New York's Greenwich Village also drew neighborhood regulars: writers, artists, and musicians. In the early sixties, new coffeehouses opened in the Village, featuring lively showcases for literary readings and folk music performances. Budding poets stood in the spotlight at the Gaslight, and James Taylor, Pete Seeger, Woody Allen, and Arlo Guthrie began their careers at the Bitter End. By the time the folk era had ended in the 1970s, so had many of these coffeehouses; the Bitter End is the last survivor.

The growing Hispanic population is a more contemporary influence on American coffee-drinking tastes. The dark roast made for the Spanish-speaking market, available on supermarket shelves everywhere, is often sought by coffee drinkers who have tired of more generic blends. In Miami, the sweet, dark coffee that traditionally fuels the Cubans' day is served all over the city, especially at simple stands where a strong brew is prepared by the filter method. In Puerto Rico, where coffee is grown, coffee-loving islanders prefer their brew dark roasted.

Americans, who consume the greatest part of the world's coffee, have come to see it as a necessary beverage at all hours of the day, its caffeine a fuel for hard workers, its very cup a magnet of sociability. Drinking coffee was once the badge of adulthood, one's first cup of coffee an important rite of passage. The rest of the world thinks we like our coffee too weak, too bland, badly made. But perhaps coffee seems undis-

The News Bar, located in Manhattan's Flatiron district, is typical of today's coffee bars, serving up light food and a wide selection of coffees.

tinguished in America because it is as ubiquitous as a glass of ice water. (In fact, coffee got iced, too; it first appeared in Philadelphia in 1876.) What Americans do like is convenience, and rejoiced when Chase and Sanborn starting selling sealed cans with ground coffee in 1878. Americans are also impatient: They took the foreign invention of freeze-drying coffee and conquered the world with a brand called Nescafé in the 1930s and made Sanka, the caffeine-free coffee from Germany, their own after General Foods introduced it sixty years ago.

By the Depression, the coffee shop had become a fixture in every town, a hangout for teenagers, a source of cheap and cheerful lunches served by waitresses wearing frilly aprons and name tags. For the most part, the coffee was mostly hot and mostly brown. Americans have been used to pairing coffee with a doughnut for dunking, a slice of pie, a crumb-covered piece of coffee cake—and drinking it almost without thinking. But now the country is in the midst of a coffee explosion. Perhaps it's because more Americans have gone to Europe and sipped the fabulous coffees there that they have grown discontent with the pallid cupful that contented for so long. Or are willing to find pleasures in simple things, well prepared at home. The national palate has improved, and though canned supermarket coffee still reigns, there is a growing culture of knowing consumers who mail-order fresh beans or visit specialty vendors, and fill their kitchens with machinery to grind and brew their beans and froth their milk. The phenomenal success of stand-up coffee bars, which began in Seattle in imitation of the espresso bars of Italy and have spread throughout the country, may be as ephemeral as many food fads, but will surely leave a more demanding coffee drinker behind.

First popularized in Seattle, gourmet coffee has become the drink of the nineties, giving rise to espresso bars nationwide. However, the essence of these bars is the same as ever: a place to relax and socialize.

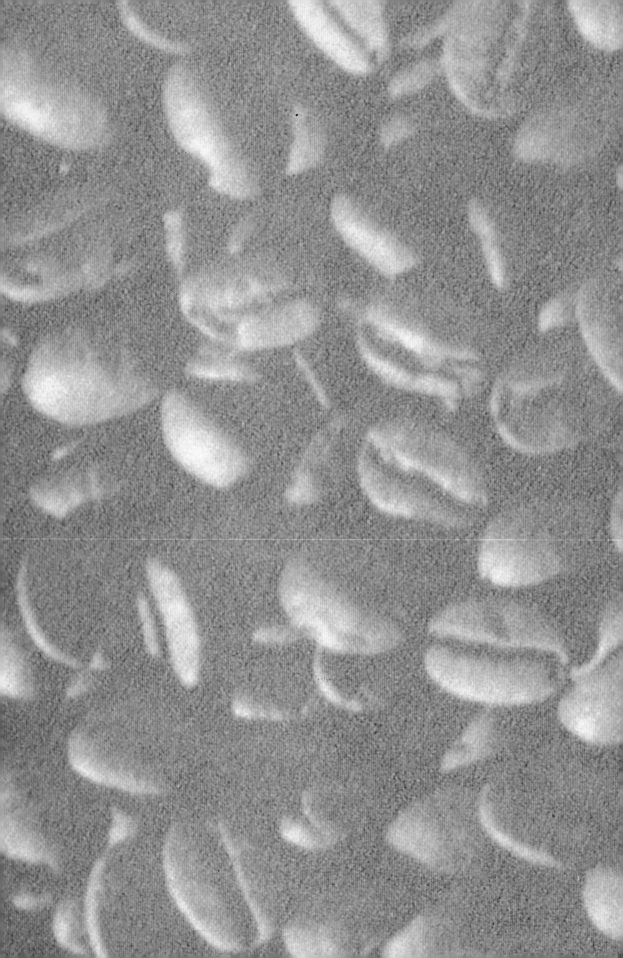

3

Coffee Lexicon

If this is coffee, please

bring me some tea;

but if this is tea, please

bring me some coffee.

—ABRAHAM LINCOLN

The Bean Scene

Most of the world's coffee is grown within a broad geographic band bordered by the Tropic of Cancer to the north and the Tropic of Capricorn to the south. Within this region, an average year-round temperature of 70 degrees Fahrenheit, with little chance of frost, and abundant rainfall provide the ideal conditions the coffee plant needs to thrive.

The species of bean grown and the method of cultivation vary from region to region and country to country. About two thirds of growers cultivate the fine-flavored, delicate *arabica*, an elongated bean that requires an altitude of 3,000 to 6,000 feet. The *robusta*, a small round bean with less refined flavor, is grown at lower altitudes and therefore is more abundant and less expensive. Nowadays beans are harvested either mechanically or by hand, depending on the steepness of the terrain and the grade of coffee. Harvesting by hand is generally the more selective method.

Much of the canned coffee that is sold in supermarkets is a blend of arabica and robusta beans. Better-

Coffee beans are the seeds contained within the bright red coffee cherry. Because cherries ripen at different rates even on the same branch, careful selection is required during harvesting.

quality coffees are often labeled according to place of origin, usually the country, such as Colombian or Brazilian. Some highly prized coffees are labeled by specific growing region, such as Jamaican Blue Mountain, and even the estate and variety of bean may be identified.

As with wine, a whole vocabulary has developed to describe and evaluate the different beans and brews. The initial indication of the freshness and quality of coffee is its *fragrance*, released first as it is roasted, then as it is ground. A lack of fragrance is a sign that a coffee is stale or past its prime. When hot water hits the grounds, tasters refer to its *aroma*, which might be described as "spicy," "fruity," or "flowery."

Well-tutored palates can distinguish the *body* of a coffee, the feel of the brew in the mouth. Tasters look for a coffee that completely "surrounds" the mouth, without overwhelming it, and might characterize a coffee as "light" or "full" or "buttery" or "syrupy."

Harvesting and processing coffee has always been a highly labor-intensive business. Here, in a nineteenth-century scene of coffee beans drying in the sun, a plantation owner supervises the stirring and turning of the precious crop for export.

Optimally, a coffee should be heavy enough to linger in the mouth a few moments after it is swallowed, though not so oily and thick that it feels as if it's coating the tongue.

The term *acidity* in relation to coffee has nothing to do with bitterness or sourness, but is rather a characteristic to be valued.

It refers to a brisk and lively quality that yields a refreshing taste to a cup and balances its richer flavors. It is the dominant characteristic of coffees grown at higher altitudes.

All these properties contribute to a coffee's *flavor.* Positive descriptions include "sweet," "bright," "fruity," or "earthy"; negatives

are "harsh," "woody," or "muddy." A "mellow" coffee is balanced, with low to medium acidity, a "mild" coffee has a delicate flavor, such as many high-grown Latin American coffees. Some coffees have a pronounced, distinguishable flavor—an Indonesian arabica has a suggestion of cardamom, for example.

The Countries

Though coffees from the same geographical area might share certain characteristics, each country, and each region within the country, tends to produce its own distinctive bean.

Brazil

For more than a century, Brazil has been the world's major coffee producer. Almost a third of the landscape is suitable for coffee cultivation. Each year the bulk of its export is the dependable, inexpensive canned coffee sold in supermarkets.

In the past, few of Brazil's coffees were distinguished by distinctive flavors, but the country is now beginning to produce excellent specialty coffees from the Bahia and Minas Gerais regions.

Colombia

The second largest exporter of coffee, Colombia produces ordinary varieties that are very good, and excellent ones that are almost unsurpassed for flavor. Arabica beans are usually grown on small farms high in the Andes, where the picking is done by hand.

Rich-tasting but light in flavor, slightly sweet, and not overly acidic, Colombia's coffee is graded by the size of the bean, either "supremo" (large beans) or "excelso" (smaller). These labels, however, are not the sole indicator of quality. As with Brazil, Colombia is beginning to produce fine coffees from a number of growing regions, including Popayan, Narino, and Bucaramanga.

Costa Rica

To some, the best-tasting Central American coffees come from Costa Rica. These sturdy beans yield a brew that has a high acidity, excellent aroma, and is well-balanced in every way. Tres Rios, Orosi, Naranjo, and Tarrazu are among the country's prominent growing regions.

As far as the eye can see, the undulating terrain of Brazil is terraced with lush coffee cultivation, which interestingly enough borders here with a crop of sugar.

Ethiopia

In this country, where the coffee tree probably originated, beans are still harvested from trees growing wild on the mountains' plateaus.

Harrar, the best known of the Ethiopian varietals, can vary widely, depending on the means of processing, ranging from rough and heavily flavored brews to top-rated cups with sweet or flowery flavors. Another varietal that has an almost fanatical following is Yrgacheffe, intensely aromatic with a distinctively rich, balanced flavor.

Guatemala

Guatemala is the source of a limited amount of top-ranked coffee, much of it grown on small farms where selectivity and careful handling are the rule. Well-balanced, mild, and richly fragrant, this coffee is especially popular in Europe and as part of espresso blends, thanks to its smoky resonance.

Using a long-handled wooden paddle, a worker gently spreads out coffee beans drying in the sun. As the sun sets, he will collect the beans into mounds to protect them from the evening moisture.

Hawaii

The first Europeans who settled the islands recognized that the warm climate and mountainous slopes were perfect for coffee plantations. Of all the islands, Kona has become the best known for the quality and distinctiveness of its crops. Small farms on the mountain of Mauna Loa, often shaded by clouds, produce coffees that entice with their rich aroma and sweet, medium-bodied flavor. Connoisseurs seek out those labeled with the names of particular estates rather than a generic "Kona" blend.

Indonesia & New Guinea

The islands of Indonesia, including Sumatra, Java, Celebes, and nearby New Guinea have been producing fine coffees for hundreds of years.

Rich and smooth, even heavy, and full of flavor, the Ankola and Mandheling coffees of Sumatra, grown at an altitude of 2,500 to 5,000 feet, are considered to be some of the world's best. The island of Celebes also produces excellent coffees with an incredibly silky texture.

Jamaica

Though the beans grown in the lowland plantations of Jamaica are not very special, those grown on Blue Mountain command a premium. Authentic Blue Mountain beans (look for certification by Jamaican Coffee Board), and not something simply labeled "Blue Mountain style," are the model of a well-tempered coffee, rich and full-bodied, balanced, aromatic, and flavorsome. Just a few hundred barrels of Blue Mountain are produced each year.

Kenya

Mt. Kenya, at an altitude of 17,000 feet, lies at the heart of the country's coffee-growing region, where banana trees are often interspersed with coffee bushes to shade the tender plants. Kenyan coffee, most of which is exported, predominantly to the United States, is smooth, with a deep flavor and the intense winy aftertaste that marks many African varietals. The "AA's" are Kenya's finest coffee.

Yemen

Mocha, one of the country's most prized coffees, is still produced by traditional methods: The trees are cultivated on rocky hillsides with careful irrigation through stone channels, and harvesting is still done by hand. Because of the dry air and soil, the small beans can be left to dry on the tree before they are picked and hulled.

The resulting flavor is unique: an almost chocolaty aftertaste, a rich and subtle sweetness, and smoothness coupled with an acidic undercurrent and distinctive aroma. Though recently in short supply, Yemen's Mocha is again reappearing on the market.

In Brazil, beans are tossed high into the air to land in wide baskets, a method of winnowing the just picked berries from any remaining leaves.

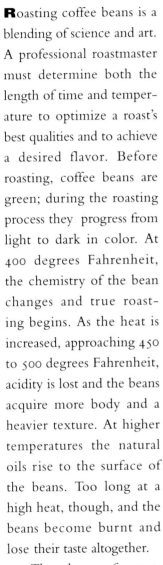

The Roasts

Roasting coffee beans is a blending of science and art. A professional roastmaster must determine both the length of time and temperature to optimize a roast's best qualities and to achieve a desired flavor. Before roasting, coffee beans are green; during the roasting process they progress from light to dark in color. At 400 degrees Fahrenheit, the chemistry of the bean changes and true roasting begins. As the heat is increased, approaching 450 to 500 degrees Fahrenheit, acidity is lost and the beans acquire more body and a heavier texture. At higher temperatures the natural oils rise to the surface of the beans. Too long at a high heat, though, and the beans become burnt and lose their taste altogether.

Though terms for roasts vary throughout the country, the following are generally accepted categories, from lightest to darkest.

American

A light roast with a very mild, sweet flavor.

Cinnamon / Vienna

This light to medium roasted coffee takes its name from the color of the bean. Used in most commercial canned coffees, it has a more intense aroma and acidity than American, though coffee lovers find it lacking in flavor.

Big / Full City

Also called regular or breakfast roast. Big City imparts a fuller body with a lighter acidity. This all-purpose roast is a popular morning coffee.

French / Continental / Spanish

A dark brown roast with beans that are quite oily and rich in flavor. French roast is often used in espresso by those who find espresso roast too burnt tasting.

Espresso

These are beans that have been roasted to nearly black in color, and are shiny with oil. Not all espresso roasts are the same: In Italy, two varieties are popular—a blond roast in the north, a dark roast in the south. Espresso contains less caffeine than any other roast.

Special Coffees

Decaffeinated coffees

It used to be that decaffeinated coffees lacked character and taste, but finding a flavorful decaffeinated coffee is becoming easier as new methods are developed for removing caffeine. There are two processes widely used today, both following the same general principle but using different solutions. Both remove over 95 percent of the caffeine.

In the traditional direct contact method, the coffee beans are soaked in warm water or steamed to bring the caffeine to the surface; treated with the solvent methylene chloride to remove the caffeine; steamed again to destroy all traces of the remaining solvent; then dried and roasted.

The second method, called the Swiss water process, repeatedly sends hot water and steam over the beans to flush away the caffeine. This process is considered more healthful by some, but for others it removes too many of the flavorful oils and results in a less distinctive cup of coffee.

Flavored coffees

Flavoring coffee can be as simple as the method used by the Belgians, who pour their coffee through a wafer of chocolate to create a cup of mocha, or the Arabs, who add cardamom or cinnamon to their brews.

During the roasting process, as the beans begin to cool down to 100 degrees Fahrenheit, they can bind with a flavoring such as amaretto, hazelnut, or chocolate, which will be released when the coffee is brewed later.

Commercial techniques in the application of flavoring have improved over the last decade, as have the flavor components. In the past, inferior-quality beans were saturated with a variety of flavorings—often of inferior quality themselves—to mask the beans' undistinctive taste. Today, the trend is toward subtle and sophisticated flavored coffees, in which all of the components are of a high quality. Popular examples run the gamut from simple chocolate, raspberry, mint, or amaretto to surprising peaches and cream.

Storing Coffee

Whatever coffee you drink, it is important to purchase and use it as fresh as possible. Unroasted coffee beans, if kept from dampness or strong odors, can be stored for up to six months before losing their quality. However, after roasting, the beans' quality will deteriorate rapidly. When the beans' fragrance is gone, your coffee has lost its freshness. For this reason, many merchants recommend buying coffee like you would buy bread: often and in small quantities.

For best results, store beans in half-pound quantities in airtight plastic bags in the freezer; use exactly what you need and grind just before brewing.

Ground coffee deteriorates even more quickly than beans. Ideally it should be purchased in very small quantities (the amount you will consume in seven days). It will stay fresh for about a week in an airtight cannister at room temperature.

Keeping ground coffee in the freezer and removing it daily is not recommended. This will cause condensation, and moisture is an enemy of coffee.

Making Your Own Blends

Once you are able to distinguish the qualities you prefer in a coffee, you might want to experiment with making your own blends. Begin with a general-purpose, reliable coffee such as a Colombian or Brazilian as a base, before adding more assertive flavors to perk up a brew. You may enjoy a spicy Sumatran coffee on its own, for example, but combining it with one or more other varieties of beans will produce even more taste complexity. You can also combine different roasts to temper the strength of a dark roast or add depth to a milder one. Professional roastmasters may add as many as a dozen beans to make a blend, but you should probably stop at three so they don't overwhelm one another.

To sweeten a blend, add Venezuelan, Haitian, or Indian coffee. Texture and fragrance are enhanced by beans from Guatemala, Kenya, and Java. New Guinea, Sumatra, or Celebes beans add richness; Central American coffees, such as those from Costa Rica, add acidity. Expensive, but adding their own "mystique" to a blend is Jamaican Blue Mountain, as well as the only coffee grown in the United States, Hawaian Kona.

The Equipment

Ibrik

This small long-handled pot, usually made of copper or brass, dates back to the origins of coffee in the Middle East and is used to make Turkish coffee: Place some coffee, ground to a powder along with sugar and water, in the pot, and bring to a boil. Remove the ibrik from the heat and stir. Repeat this twice before serving the thick and syrupy brew.

Cafetiere

A simple design that dates from the 1920s, the cafetiere, or plunger pot, makes a rich brew, as oils are not removed by a paper filter. Place medium-ground coffee in the pot, pour hot water over it, and allow to steep for five minutes. Then press the plunger to separate the coffee and force the grounds to the bottom of the pot.

Neapolitan Flip Drip

Also called café filtre or machinetta. Put cold water in the bottom half of the pot, and fine-ground coffee in the filter basket. When the water boils the steam will begin to escape from the hole below the basket. Remove the pot from the heat and flip it over. The hot water will trickle through the grounds to make the coffee.

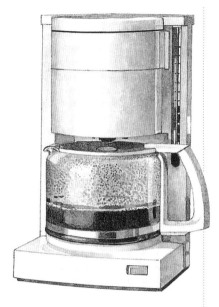

Moka Espresso Pot

This is a simple non-electric espresso maker. Place cold water in the bottom of the pot, measure coffee in the basket in the middle, and screw the pot together. Heat just until a hiss signals that steam forced up from the bottom through the grounds to the upper chamber has condensed as coffee.

Filter Method

In the simplest version of the filter method, fit a paper filter into a cone, fill it with fine-ground coffee, and trickle hot water into the cone until the desired amount of coffee appears in the pot. In an electric drip maker, hot water is automatically heated and dripped through the coffee into a pot that sits on a warming plate. Depending on whether the coffee is in a cone or a basket, use a fine or medium grind.

Percolator

Popular in the 1940s and 1950s. With this brewing method, the water is heated, then forced up through a center tube and constantly circulated over the bed of coarse ground coffee. Because water is repeatedly run over the coffee, over-extraction often occurs, diminishing the freshness and flavor.

The Grinds

Choose the type of grind according to the method of coffee preparation you are using. In general, the coarser the grind, the longer the coffee must remain in contact with water. The finer the grind, the more quickly the essential elements—fragrance, aroma and flavor—will be released. Espresso, for instance, which requires only 20 to 30 seconds for brewing, needs a finely ground coffee; the filter method, which takes much longer, requires a medium or fine grind for proper extraction.

It can be difficult to grind beans uniformly in an electric or hand mill at home. Having your coffee merchant grind your beans when you buy them will generally give you a more exact calibration of beans to pot. Here are some typical grinds:

Coarse

Used for percolators as well as the old-fashioned boiled method.

Medium

Used for plunger pots and electric drip method with basket-type filters where the water is in contact with the grounds for a longer period of time.

Fine

This is the grind for Neapolitan flip drip pots and Melitta filter cones.

Extra-Fine

Used for espresso and Turkish coffee. Stop and start the machine several times when grinding for a long time, so that you do not heat the coffee, and tap it to distribute the grounds.

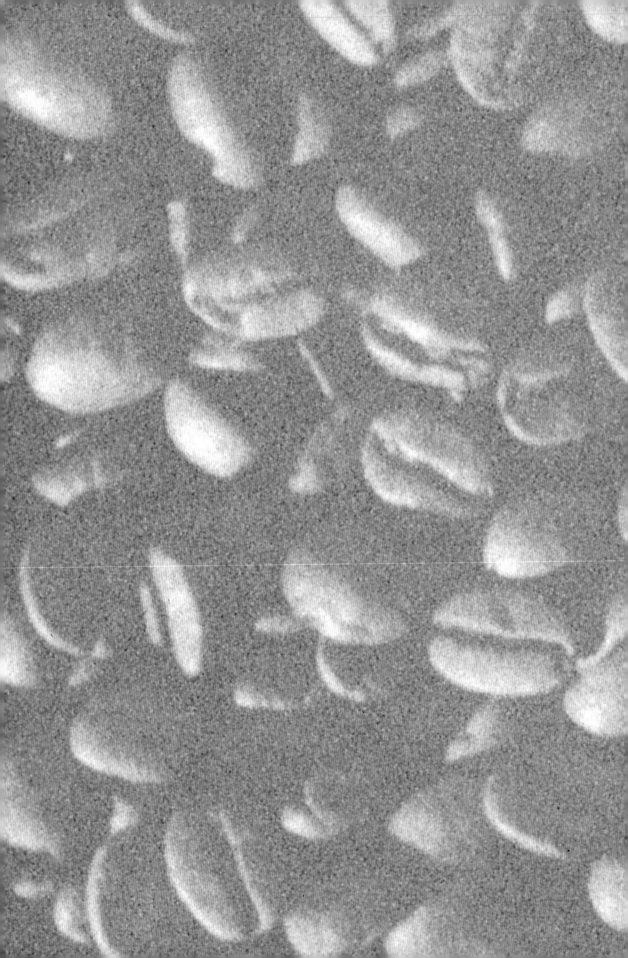

CHAPTER 4

Recipes

The best maxim I know

in life, is to drink your

coffee when you can,

and when you cannot,

to be easy without it.

—JONATHAN SWIFT

Recipes

· ·

THERE IS AS MUCH VARIATION IN COFFEE drinkers themselves as there is in coffee beans, roasts, grinds, and methods of brewing. Some people roast their own organic beans and drink only French-pressed or plunger-pot coffee. Others enjoy a flavored blend in a fancy mug, or sweetened espresso in a demitasse. Most brew coffee by the electric filter drip method. There is no right way; ultimately it is a matter of personal taste. However, some guidelines, both general and specific follow for making the best coffee or espresso drinks with whatever equipment you prefer.

Coffee beans are perishable and should be used as quickly as possible. Store them in airtight containers at room temperature, not in the freezer or refrigerator. To get the freshest flavor from the beans, always grind them just before use. Use the proper grind for the method of brewing (page 59). Too fine a grind will clog a filter or make your coffee muddy with coffee particles. Too coarse a grind will produce weak, bitter coffee.

Always brew coffee with fresh cold water and only use water you would drink. If you think the water does not taste good, don't brew coffee with it. Use bottled water instead.

Use at least 2 tablespoons of coffee for each 5- to 6-ounce cup. (Most mugs hold more, so you may want to use up to 3 tablespoons of ground coffee per mug.) Brewing coffee too weak is the most common error people make. Strong coffee allows the flavor of the bean to become distinct. You can always add more hot water to the cup if your coffee is too strong (see Espresso Americano, page 78).

To make espresso or cappuccino, you will need either an electric espresso machine or stovetop espresso maker equipped with a valve for steaming milk or a special stovetop device just for steaming milk. Creating the perfect foam or froth is not the same or as simple as heating the milk; in fact, the milk is frothed first and then heated. Cold milk froths best, hot milk will not froth at all. Follow the manufacturer's suggestions for these techniques, and remember that practice often makes perfect, but even less than perfect tastes good.

Use whole milk and fresh heavy cream where these ingredients are called for, but if you prefer low-fat or skimmed milk, these will froth just as well—some coffee drinkers say better.

The terms for coffee and espresso drinks tend to blur and overlap one another: One person's *latte* is another's *café au lait*. All the recipes in this section, including the food, can be made with decaffeinated coffee without any compromise in flavor as long as you buy good-quality fresh beans.

About the recipes: Just as coffee has no "proper" time or place, the list of foods that pair well with the beverage seems to go on and on. What follows is a selection of dishes that shows off coffee's glorious affinity for a wide variety of flavors and foods: sweet and savory baked goods for breakfast; soups, sandwiches, and salads for lunch; even surprisingly hearty fare for dinner; and of course wonderful desserts and sweet snacks at any time of the day. Also included are coffee drinks, from steaming hot to ice cold, decaffeinated to deliciously spiked. Coffee never had so many wonderful partners.

Hot Coffee

Café au Lait or Café con Leche

For each serving

6 ounces steamed milk

6 ounces freshly brewed strong hot coffee (French roast)

Cocoa, freshly grated nutmeg, or cinnamon, for dusting (optional)

Pour the steamed milk and coffee simultaneously into a warmed café au lait bowl or large coffee cup. Dust the top with cocoa, nutmeg, or cinnamon, if desired. Serve steaming hot.

Viennese Coffee

"VIENNESE COFFEE" ALMOST ALWAYS MEANS COFFEE WITH WHIPPED CREAM AND, WHEN PRESENTED AUTHENTICALLY, WILL BE SERVED IN 5- TO 6-OUNCE STEMMED CLEAR GLASSES.

For each serving

4 to **5** ounces freshly brewed hot coffee (Full City roast)

Softly whipped cream, for serving

Cinnamon, cloves, or freshly grated nutmeg, for dusting (optional)

Pour the coffee into a stemmed glass and top with a dollop of whipped cream. Dust the cream with ground cinnamon, cloves, or nutmeg, if desired. Serve at once.

Café Belgique

THIS COMBINATION MAY ALSO BE CALLED COFFEE WITH WHIPPED EGG WHITES. IN SOME INSTANCES, WHIPPED CREAM IS FOLDED INTO THE EGG WHITES. ENJOY A CUP OF THIS IN THE LATE AFTERNOON.

For each serving

1 large egg white

1/2 teaspoon vanilla extract

4 to **5** ounces freshly brewed hot coffee (Full City or French roast)

1 to **2** tablespoons half-and-half

In a small bowl, whip the egg white with the vanilla until stiff. Place a generous tablespoon of whipped egg white into the bottom of a cup. Pour the hot coffee into the cup and add the half-and-half. The egg white will rise to the top. Serve at once.

NOTE: One beaten egg white will be enough for 3 to 4 cups of coffee.

Spiced Coffee

ANY FILTER METHOD OF BREWING COFFEE IS THE WAY TO MAKE THIS FLAVORFUL BLEND. THINK OF THIS AS A DESSERT-TYPE COFFEE. FOR VARIATION, REPLACE THE NUTMEG WITH 1/4 TEASPOON GROUND CARDAMOM. THE AMOUNT OF SPICES BELOW WILL BE ENOUGH FOR 3 TO 4 CUPS.

8 whole cloves

1/4 teaspoon freshly grated nutmeg

1 cinnamon stick

One 3 to 4-inch strip orange zest

One 3-inch strip lemon zest

Place the spices and citrus zests in the bottom of a filter-drip coffee pot. Brew the coffee as usual, letting it drip onto the spices. Strain before serving hot.

Coffee with Chocolate

CAFÉ MOCHA, STRICTLY SPEAKING, IS
MADE WITH ESPRESSO RATHER THAN
REGULAR COFFEE. BUT CHOCOLATE AND
COFFEE, REGARDLESS OF ITS STRENGTH,
ALWAYS MAKE A GREAT COMBINATION.
(FOR THE CLASSIC VERSION, SEE PAGE 80.)

For each serving

5 to **6** ounces freshly brewed hot coffee
(French roast)

1/3 cup chocolate milk, heated

Softly whipped cream, for serving

Cocoa or grated bittersweet chocolate, for
dusting

In a mug, stir together the coffee and the chocolate milk. Top with a spoonful of whipped cream and garnish with cocoa or bittersweet chocolate. Serve at once.

Irish Coffee

OF ALL THE FLAVORED HOT COFFEES, IRISH
COFFEE, FAMOUS FOR ITS ABILITY TO
WARM YOUR INSIDES AND YOUR SPIRIT, IS
THE FIRST THAT COMES TO MIND. TO BE
REALLY AUTHENTIC, IT SHOULD BE SERVED
IN STEMMED CLEAR GLASSES.

For each serving

1 teaspoon sugar

4 to **5** ounces freshly brewed hot coffee

1 ounce Irish whiskey or Scotch

Softly whipped cream, for serving

Place the sugar in the bottom of an Irish coffee glass and pour in the coffee. Add the Irish whiskey and top with a tablespoon of whipped cream. Serve immediately.

Cardamom and Orange Coffee

USE ETHIOPIAN HARRAR OR ANOTHER SIMILAR BEAN AND A PLUNGER POT OR THE FRENCH PRESS METHOD FOR BREWING THIS DENSELY FLAVORED DESSERT DRINK.

For 2 servings

Ethiopian Harrar coffee

1/2 teaspoon freshly ground cardamom seeds

The zest of 1 orange, removed in strips with a vegetable peeler

Raw or brown sugar, for serving

In the coffee pot, combine the coffee grounds, cardamom, and orange zest. Add enough boiling water for 2 servings and let the coffee brew for about 4 minutes before depressing the plunger.

Sweeten to taste with raw or brown sugar. Serve immediately in small coffee cups.

Café Midnight

For each serving

1 1/2 tablespoons crème de cacao

1 1/2 tablespoons Sambuca

Freshly brewed strong hot coffee (French roast)

Softly whipped cream, for serving

Into a coffee mug or cup, pour the crème de cacao and the Sambuca. Add the hot coffee and top with a dollop of the whipped cream. Serve at once.

Espresso Drinks

Straight Espresso

A true espresso, known as a straight, is served in a warmed demitasse (3-ounce capacity) with a saucer and a small demitasse spoon. The standard serving size is 1½ ounces, filling the cup only half way. Each serving is made with about 2 tablespoons of ground espresso beans. Espresso is dark in color, crowned by a foam, and full in flavor. If you want to sweeten espresso, do—with sugar.

Espresso Romano

This is straight espresso served with a twist of lemon—yellow peel only—on the side. Occasionally orange or tangerine peel is substituted. Twist the citrus peel to release the oils in it before adding it to the hot espresso for flavor.

A short pull is 1 ounce of espresso served in a demitasse.

An espresso lungo uses 2 tablespoons of ground espresso beans but a larger amount of water than usual to produce an almost 3-ounce serving of espresso—a less-than-full-strength cup.

A double espresso, or *dóppio* in Italian, uses double the standard measure of ground espresso and water to produce 3 ounces of espresso—in essence two servings.

An espresso Americano is a single serving of espresso (1½ ounces) diluted with an additional 3 to 4 ounces hot water, served in a regular coffee cup.

An espresso macchiato is a single serving of espresso (1½ ounces) just "marked" with a touch of steamed milk, served in a demitasse.

An espresso con panna is a single serving of espresso (1½ ounces) topped with whipped cream, served in a demitasse.

On a final note, flavorings, whether they are simple extracts (usually vanilla, almond, or orange) or flavored fountain syrups, are not usually added to straight espresso, but are more commonly added to espresso drinks (those to which steamed milk has been added).

Caffè Latte

The drink that has most recently become all the rage here hasn't much of a following in Italy. Generally speaking, a latte is a single serving of espresso (1½ ounces) poured simultaneously with steamed milk (4 to 6 ounces) into a tall glass. Lattes can be garnished with ground cinnamon, nutmeg, or sweetened chocolate powder.

Popular flavored lattes contain 1 to 2 tablespoons of fountain syrup added to the drink after it is made. Almond, hazelnut, orange, vanilla, chocolate, anisette, crème de menthe, and chocolate mint are just some of the flavors available. Specialty coffee shops usually have a range of these flavored syrups from which you can choose.

You can also use regular flavoring extracts—pure or imitation—such as almond, vanilla, rum, mint, or orange to flavor any espresso or coffee drink.

Pure extract has a stronger flavor than an imitation extract: If using a pure extract, start with ⅛ to ¼ teaspoon pure extract per serving; double that (¼ to ½ teaspoon) if using an imitation extract. Increase the amount to suit your taste.

Latte Macchiato

This is a tall glass of steamed and frothed milk to which espresso is added by dribbling or dripping it through the froth. The amount of espresso can vary from 1 to 3 tablespoons.

Cappuccino

Many so-called cappuccinos suffer from the addition of too much milk and even ice-cream parlor toppings such as cherries, sprinkles, and flavored chocolate powder dustings. A traditional cappuccino is served in a 6-ounce cup and consists of a serving of espresso (1½ ounces) to which about the same amount of frothed milk is added. Properly prepared froth is dense, not stiff like meringue, and should barely reach the top edge of the cup.

If you want to flavor your cappuccino, do so sparingly, starting with 1 teaspoon of flavored fountain syrup. Let the simple flavor of the espresso come through the steamed milk.

C   O   F   F   E   E

Café Mocha

LIKE FLAVORED LATTES, CAFÉ MOCHA CAN ALSO INCLUDE OTHER FOUNTAIN SYRUPS OR EXTRACTS, SUCH AS HAZELNUT, ALMOND, MINT, OR ORANGE.

For each serving

1 to **2** tablespoons chocolate syrup

1 serving (1 1/2 ounces) fresh hot espresso

2 ounces steamed milk

Softly whipped cream, for serving (optional)

Coat the inside of a 5- to 6-ounce coffee cup or mug with the chocolate syrup. Pour in the espresso and then the steamed milk, and top with a tablespoon or 2 of whipped cream, if desired.

NOTE: For a richer chocolate flavor, substitute 1 to 2 tablespoons Bittersweet Chocolate Sauce (page 142) for the chocolate syrup above.

Brève

THIS ESPRESSO DRINK IS MADE WITH STEAMED HALF-AND-HALF INSTEAD OF MILK. ITS RICHER TASTE MAKES IT DEFINITELY WORTH TRYING.

For each serving

1 serving (1 1/2 ounces) fresh hot espresso

1 to **3** ounces steamed half-and-half

Pour the espresso into a warmed 5- to 6-ounce coffee cup and add steamed half-and-half to taste.

Iced Coffees and Espressos

Some coffee drinkers only like their coffee iced, perhaps because iced coffee seems to have a smooth, less-bitter taste. Here are a few suggestions that will result in fresh-tasting delicious iced coffee drinks.

• Brew coffee to be used in iced drinks double strength to allow for the ice melting and diluting the drink. (If you are using espresso as the base of the iced drink, this is not necessary.)

• Brewed coffee or espresso held in the refrigerator for more than half a day will not taste as bright or flavorful as fresh, but it will work just fine in a pinch.

• To chill hot coffee or espresso, use crushed ice rather than cubes. Ice chips cool hot coffee more quickly without diluting its flavor as much. Crush ice cubes by wrapping them loosely in a clean dish towel and pounding them on a hard surface with a hammer.

• Another option to consider for chilling iced drinks is to make coffee ice cubes. This is especially useful when making pitchers of iced coffee for large gatherings. Start by making double-strength coffee, cooling it, and then pouring it into to ice-cube trays. Freeze and use the cubes as you would regular ice cubes. Or crush them, as described above.

• Use cold milk rather than hot frothed milk where recipes call for milk.

• If you want froth or foam on the top of an iced drink, froth milk and scoop only the froth onto the cold drink.

• Dissolve sugar for sweetening iced coffee drinks in hot coffee or espresso, if possible. Sugar is more difficult to dissolve in cold liquid.

Four O'Clock Iced Coffee

For each serving

Crushed iced

1 serving (1 1/2 ounces) fresh hot espresso (optional)

1 cup freshly brewed strong hot coffee

1 teaspoon vanilla extract

1/4 cup half-and-half

Fill a tall glass with crushed ice. Pour in the espresso, if desired, the coffee, vanilla, and half-and-half. Stir and serve.

Spiced Espresso Shake

For each serving

1 double serving (3 ounces) espresso or 1/2 cup freshly brewed double-strength coffee, chilled

1 scoop honey vanilla, coffee, or chocolate ice cream

1/4 cup cold milk

Softly whipped cream, for serving

Cinnamon, for dusting

Combine the espresso, ice cream, and cold milk in a blender. Blend for 15 to 20 seconds, or until smooth. Pour into a chilled glass and top with a spoonful or 2 of whipped cream and a dusting of cinnamon.

Iced Amaretto Espresso

A VERY NICE VARIATION ON THIS SIMPLY DOUBLES THE AMOUNT OF ESPRESSO. OR USE THE SAME AMOUNT OF ESPRESSO SUGGESTED BELOW BUT SUBSTITUTE 1/2 CUP CLUB SODA FOR THE MILK, AND SERVE GARNISHED WITH A SLICE OF ORANGE.

For each serving

Crushed ice

1 serving (1 1/2 ounces) fresh hot espresso

1 ounce amaretto

1/2 cup cold milk

Fill a rocks glass half full with crushed ice. Add the espresso, then the amaretto, and finally the cold milk. Stir and serve.

Smoked Salmon and Herb Omelettes

THESE OMELETTES — MINUS THE SALMON — CAN ALSO BE SERVED WITH VARIOUS TOPPINGS. SLIT THEM DOWN THE CENTER, SET OUT SMALL BOWLS OF SHREDDED SWISS CHEESE, CRUMBLED BACON, SOUR CREAM, AND SAUTÉED MUSHROOMS AND LET YOUR FAMILY OR GUESTS CREATE THEIR OWN. THEY ARE A NATURAL FOR BRUNCH OR AS A LIGHT SUPPER WITH GOOD BREAD AND A TASTY SALAD.

2 tablespoons finely chopped fresh basil

2 tablespoons finely chopped fresh chives

2 tablespoons finely chopped fresh parsley

2 teaspoons finely chopped fresh thyme or rosemary

1/2 cup diced smoked salmon

12 large eggs

3 tablespoons unsalted butter

Salt and freshly ground black pepper

In a small bowl, combine all the fresh herbs.

For each omelette: In a bowl, whisk together 3 of the eggs and a quarter of the mixed fresh herbs. Stir in 2 tablespoons smoked salmon.

Heat 2 teaspoons of the butter in a well-seasoned 8-inch omelette pan until hot and bubbly. Add the herbed eggs and cook over medium-high heat, shaking the pan and stirring with a fork, without scraping the bottom of the pan, until the eggs begin to set. Tilt the pan and pull the cooked egg to the center to allow the uncooked egg to run underneath and set quickly on the hot surface. When the edges of the omelette are cooked and the center is soft but not runny, fold the edges of the omelette in toward the center, roughly in thirds. Remove the pan from the heat and turn the folded omelette, folded side down, out onto a warm serving plate. Season to taste with salt and pepper and serve at once. Make 3 more omelettes with the remaining butter, herbs, salmon, and eggs in the same manner.

Makes 4 servings

Scrambled Egg, Potato, and Green Chile Burritos

BURRITOS ARE THE SIMPLEST FORM OF SOUTHWESTERN COOKING. LIKE SANDWICHES, THEY WORK WITH LEFTOVERS OR WHATEVER INGREDIENTS YOU HAVE ON HAND. SO IF GREEN CHILE AND CILANTRO AREN'T YOUR FAVORITE FLAVORS, TRY CHOPPED RED BELL PEPPER AND BASIL INSTEAD.

For the Green Chile Salsa (Makes 1 cup)

1/2 onion, chopped

1/2 green bell pepper, seeded and chopped

2 garlic cloves

3 tablespoons olive oil

1/4 cup roasted green chile, fresh or frozen and thawed, peeled, seeded, and chopped (see Note)

1/2 teaspoon cumin

Juice of 1 lime

2 tablespoons chopped cilantro

1/2 teaspoon chopped fresh oregano or a pinch of dried

Salt and freshly ground black pepper

4 large eggs, softly scrambled

3 all-purpose potatoes, cut into medium dice and boiled or panfried until tender

4 large (10-inch) flour tortillas

4 ounces Monterey Jack cheese, shredded

For garnish

Sour cream

Chopped cilantro

Chopped scallions

Preheat the oven to 350°F.

Prepare the Green Chile Salsa: In a skillet, sauté the onion, green bell pepper, and garlic in the olive oil until the onion and bell pepper soften slightly. Transfer the vegetables to a food processor fitted with a metal blade and add all the remaining salsa ingredients except the salt and pepper. Pulse several times, for 3 to 5 seconds only, until the ingredients are combined but still chunky. Add salt and pepper to taste. Pour the salsa into a serving bowl and set it aside at room temperature.

Assemble the burritos: Put an equal amount of the eggs and potatoes in the center of each tortilla. Top with 2 table-spoons of the salsa and divide the shredded cheese among them. Roll up each tortilla, enclosing the filling, and wrap each one securely in foil. Bake for 15 to 20 minutes.

Unwrap the burritos and transfer to heated plates. Top each burrito with additional salsa and garnish as desired.

Makes 4 servings

Scrambled Egg,
Potato, and Green Chile
Burritos

Fresh Pineapple,
Banana, and Papaya
Fruit Salad

Sour Cream Coffee Cake
(PAGE 94)

Coffee with Chocolate
(page 76)

Hot Couscous Cereal
with Honey
(PAGE 96)

Blackberry Apple
Muffins
(PAGE 89)

Café au Lait
(PAGE 74)

NOTE: In New Mexico, when we say green chile, we mean Hatch or New Mexican green chiles, which are long, smooth-skinned, firm peppers available fresh at any grocery store from September through November and frozen year-round. They are mild to hot and vary in strength, depending on the weather of the growing year.

During their season they are sold by the bushel or burlap bag and roasted in wire barrels over gas flames. I invite friends over and equip them with plastic gloves, and we sit in the yard, sip coffee, and peel and seed chiles. The heat, I've finally learned, is not in the seeds, but in the veins, which can be pulled off carefully. Sometimes we chop the chiles or cut them into strips; other times we leave them whole for stuffing. We bag them in small quantities to freeze and use them throughout the year.

If Hatch chiles are not available, omit the chopped bell pepper in the salsa and add 1 green bell pepper, roasted (see page 103 for procedure), seeded, and chopped.

Black Bean, Feta, and Red Salsa Burritos

SMOOTH CREAMY BLACK BEANS STAND UP WELL TO THE SALTY BITE OF FETA CHEESE AND RICH ROASTED GARLIC. WE EAT THESE BURRITOS ON A REGULAR BASIS, AND I OFTEN LIKE TO SUBSTITUTE GOAT CHEESE FOR THE FETA. TAKE THE TIME TO ROAST YOUR OWN GARLIC—ITS NUTTY TASTE IS MILDER THAN THAT OF FRESH GARLIC, AND IT IS DELICIOUS SPREAD ON TOASTED BREAD OR CRACKERS, IN SALAD DRESSINGS, OR IN MASHED POTATOES.

For the red salsa (Makes 1 cup)

1/2 red onion, coarsely chopped

2 tablespoons olive oil

3 Roma tomatoes, quartered

3 sun-dried tomatoes, packed in oil, drained, and chopped

3 garlic cloves, roasted (see Note)

1 tablespoon finely chopped cilantro

Juice of 1 lemon

2 teaspoons mild to medium-hot pure ground New Mexican red chile (available at some gourmet food stores) or **1** teaspoon chili powder

2 teaspoons red wine vinegar

Salt and freshly ground black pepper

One 16-ounce can refried black beans

4 large (10-inch) flour tortillas

4 ounces feta cheese, crumbled

For garnish

Sour cream

Chopped scallions

Chopped cilantro

Lime wedges

Preheat the oven to 350°F.

Prepare the red salsa: In a small pan, cook the onion in the olive oil over medium heat until it softens slightly. Transfer to a food processor fitted with the metal blade and add all the remaining salsa ingredients except the salt and pepper. Pulse several times, for 3 to 5 seconds only, until the ingredients are combined but still chunky. Add salt and pepper to taste. Pour the salsa into a serving bowl and set it aside at room temperature.

Assemble the burritos: Put an equal amount of the refried black beans in the center of each tortilla. Top with the crumbled feta and 2 to 3 tablespoons of the salsa. Roll up each tortilla and wrap securely in foil. Bake for 15 to 20 minutes.

Unwrap the burritos and transfer to heated plates. Top with additional salsa, a dollop of sour cream, scallions, and cilantro, and garnish each plate with lime wedges.

Makes 4 servings

NOTE: To roast garlic, place a whole unpeeled head in a small baking dish and drizzle it with about 2 tablespoons olive oil. Cover tightly and bake in a preheated 375°F. oven for 20 to 30 minutes. The cloves should yield easily when poked beneath their papery skins. Let cool, cut the tops off, and you will be able to squeeze the soft whole cloves right out of their skins.

Black Bean, Plantain, and Jalapeño Burritos

For the salsa, substitute the juice of 2 limes for the lemon juice and omit the red wine vinegar. Omit the ground red chili and add 2 finely chopped jalapeño chile peppers, fresh or canned.

For the burritos, omit the feta cheese. Cut 2 plantains into ¼-inch slices. In a small sauté pan, heat 3 tablespoons butter until bubbly, add the plantains, and cook over medium heat, stirring often, for about 10 minutes, until soft.

Assemble the burritos according to the directions above, adding 4 or 5 slices of cooked plantains to each one in place of the feta cheese. Roll up and heat the burritos as directed above.

Cornmeal Muffins with Raspberries

THE CORNMEAL SUPPLIES THE CRUNCHINESS AND THE RASPBERRIES THE SWEETNESS, WHICH TOGETHER MAKE FOR AN INTERESTING CONTRAST IN THESE HARD-TO-RESIST MUFFINS. FOR A SAVORY VARIATION, ONE THAT WOULD BE GOOD WITH SPICY SWEET POTATO SOUP (PAGE 97) OR WITH CHILI CON CARNE (PAGE 132), OMIT THE RASPBERRIES AND DECREASE THE SUGAR TO 2 TABLESPOONS.

1 1/2 cups yellow cornmeal

1 cup all-purpose flour

1/3 cup sugar

1 tablespoon baking powder

1 1/2 teaspoons baking soda

2 large eggs

1 cup buttermilk

1/2 cup milk

5 tablespoons unsalted butter, melted

1 cup fresh or frozen raspberries

Preheat the oven to 375°F. Line a 12-cup muffin tin with paper or foil baking cups or generously grease the muffin cups.

In a bowl, stir together the cornmeal, flour, sugar, baking powder, and baking soda; set aside.

In a medium bowl, combine the eggs, buttermilk, milk, and melted butter, whisking until smooth. Pour the wet ingredients into the dry ones, stirring lightly 2 or 3 times, and add the raspberries. Continue to stir the batter only until just combined. Do not overmix, or the muffins will be tough.

Spoon the batter into the prepared cups, filling each about three-quarters full. Bake the muffins for 20 to 25 minutes, until the edges of the muffins pull slightly away from the sides of the pan and the tops spring back when lightly touched. Let the muffins cool in the tin for several minutes, then transfer them to a wire rack to cool completely.

Makes 12 muffins

Cornmeal Muffins with Fresh Rosemary

Omit the raspberries and stir 2 teaspoons finely chopped fresh rosemary into the batter. Bake as directed above.

Blackberry Apple Muffins

WHOLE BLACKBERRIES CAN SOMETIMES BE A BIT LARGE FOR THESE MUFFINS. WHEN THEY ARE, THEY DON'T BAKE PROPERLY, SO I CUT THEM INTO TWO OR THREE SMALLER PIECES. THESE ARE A HIT WITH KIDS, AND THEY'RE ALSO GREAT IN THE MORNING WITH A FRESH CUP OF *CAFÉ AU LAIT*.

1 Granny Smith apple, peeled, cored, and coarsely chopped

3/4 cup blackberries, fresh or frozen and thawed, coarsely chopped

2 cups all-purpose flour

2/3 cup sugar

2 teaspoons baking powder

1/2 teaspoon baking soda

1/2 teaspoon cinnamon

2 large eggs

4 tablespoons (1/2 stick) unsalted butter, melted

1 cup sour cream

1/2 cup milk

Preheat the oven to 375°F. Line a 12-cup muffin tin with paper or foil baking cups or generously grease the muffin cups.

In a bowl, toss the apple and blackberries together with 2 tablespoons of the flour. Into another bowl, sift together the remaining flour, the sugar, baking powder, baking soda, and cinnamon; set aside.

In a medium bowl, combine the eggs, butter, sour cream, and milk, whisking until smooth. Pour the wet ingredients into the dry ones, stirring lightly 2 or 3 times, and add the blackberry mixture. Continue to stir only until just combined. Do not overmix, or the muffins will be tough.

Spoon the batter into the prepared cups, filling each cup at least three-quarters full. Bake the muffins for 22 to 25 minutes, until the edges of the muffins pull slightly away from the sides of the pan and the tops spring back when lightly touched. Let the muffins cool in the tin for several minutes, then transfer them to a wire rack to cool completely.

Makes 12 muffins

Onion, Parmesan, and Prosciutto Muffins

ALTHOUGH THESE ARE SAVORY MUFFINS, THE ONION IN THE BATTER ADDS A SURPRISINGLY SWEET NOTE. PAIRED WITH A FRESH GREEN SALAD, THESE FLAVORFUL MUFFINS CAN ALSO MAKE A SATISFYING LIGHT LUNCH. IF PROSCIUTTO IS UNAVAILABLE AT YOUR MARKET, SUBSTITUTE CRUMBLED COOKED BACON.

2 cups all-purpose flour

2 teaspoons baking powder

1/2 teaspoon baking soda

3/4 cup freshly grated Parmesan cheese

1/3 cup chopped thinly sliced prosciutto

2 large eggs

1/2 cup sour cream

3/4 cup milk

1 tablespoon honey

1 tablespoon olive oil

1 1/2 teaspoons finely chopped fresh rosemary

1 teaspoon finely chopped fresh thyme

1/2 medium onion, chopped

4 tablespoons (1/2 stick) unsalted butter, melted

Preheat the oven to 375°F. Line a 12-cup muffin tin with paper or foil baking cups or generously grease the muffin cups.

Into a bowl, sift together the flour, baking powder, and baking soda. Stir in the Parmesan cheese and prosciutto; set aside.

In another bowl, combine the eggs, sour cream, milk, honey, olive oil, rosemary, thyme, onion, and butter, whisking until the mixture is combined. Pour the wet ingredients into the dry ones, stirring the batter only until just combined. Do not overmix or the muffins will be tough.

Spoon the batter into the prepared cups, filling each at least three-quarters full. Bake the muffins for 20 to 25 minutes, until the edges of the muffins pull slightly away from the sides of the pan and the tops spring back when lightly touched. Let the muffins cool in the tin for several minutes, then transfer them to a wire rack to cool completely.

Makes 12 muffins

Frangipane Crescents

MAKING YOUR OWN CROISSANT DOUGH IS FUN BUT TIME-CONSUMING. THESE ALMOND-FILLED PASTRIES USE COMMERCIALLY MADE DOUGH WHICH IS THE NEXT BEST THING. BECAUSE THEY CAN BE PUT TOGETHER QUICKLY, YOU CAN MAKE THEM ON ALMOST ANY MORNING. FOR AN EASY VARIATION, FORGO THE FRANGIPANE AND SPREAD EACH TRIANGLE WITH A TEASPOON OR TWO OF YOUR FAVORITE JAM.

For the frangipane filling

2 tablespoons unsalted butter, softened

2 ounces almond paste, crumbled

1/4 cup sugar

1/2 cup almonds, coarsely ground

1 large egg yolk

One 8-ounce tube crescent roll dough
  (such as Pillsbury)

Preheat the oven to 375°F.

Prepare the filling: In a food processor fitted with a metal blade, combine all the frangipane filling ingredients. Pulse several times until all the ingredients are combined but the filling is still lumpy.

Remove the crescent roll dough from the tube and separate it into triangles. Place 1 tablespoon of the filling on the widest end of each triangle, leaving the edges uncovered. Roll into crescents according to the directions on the package. Transfer the crescents to an ungreased baking sheet, leaving 1½ inches in between, and bake them for 12 to 15 minutes. Transfer the crescents to a wire rack to cool slightly.

Makes eight 4-inch crescents

Frangipane- and Chocolate-Filled Crescents

Place 1 tablespoon of the frangipane filling on the widest end of each triangle of dough, and top it with 5 chocolate chips. Roll and bake as directed above.

Chocolate Crescents

Omit the frangipane filling, and place 8 or 10 semisweet chocolate chips in the center of the widest end of each triangle of dough. Roll and bake as directed above.

Orange Poppy Seed Scones

THE SECRET TO MAKING GOOD—MEANING LIGHT—SCONES LIES IN THE PROPER HANDLING OF THE DOUGH: OVERWORKING IT WILL CAUSE THE SCONES TO BECOME TOUGH; TOO LITTLE HANDLING AND THE SCONES WILL FALL APART AS THEY BAKE. ANOTHER TIP TO REMEMBER IS TO REMOVE THE SCONES FROM THE OVEN WHILE THEY'RE STILL QUITE SOFT IN THE CENTER, SO THEY WON'T DRY OUT AS THEY COOL.

2 1/2 cups all-purpose flour

6 tablespoons sugar

3/4 teaspoon baking powder

3/4 teaspoon baking soda

1/4 teaspoon salt

1 tablespoon poppy seeds

10 tablespoons cold unsalted butter, cut into tablespoon-sized pieces

3/4 cup buttermilk

1 tablespoon grated orange zest

Preheat the oven to 375°F. Grease a baking sheet.

In a medium-size bowl, combine the flour, sugar, baking powder, baking soda, salt, and poppy seeds. Using a pastry blender or 2 knives, cut the cold butter into the dry ingredients until the dough is crumbly and the butter is the size of coarse crumbs. Add the buttermilk and orange zest and stir lightly until the dough is combined and comes together to form a ball. (The dough will be slightly crumbly and dry.)

On a lightly floured surface, roll or pat the dough into a 12-inch circle about 1 inch thick. Cut the dough into 8 wedges. With a spatula, transfer the wedges to the prepared baking sheet and bake them for 22 to 25 minutes, or until the edges are lightly browned but the centers are still soft. Transfer the scones to a wire rack to cool. Serve warm or at room temperature, preferably on the day they are made.

Makes 8 scones

Smoked Salmon
and Herb Omelettes
(PAGE 83)

Orange Poppy Seed
Scones

Sweet Butter
and Apricot Preserves

Fresh Honeydew
Melon and Grapefruit
Sections with Lime

Cafè Latte
(PAGE 79)

Crab-Stuffed
French Toast
(PAGE 109)

Pan-Fried Potatoes and
Crumbled Bacon

Sliced Orange Salad

Currant and Walnut
Biscotti
(PAGE 113)

Spiced Coffee
(PAGE 75)

Sun-Dried Cherry and Oatmeal Scones

Decrease the amount of flour to 2 cups and omit the poppy seeds and orange zest. Add ½ cup quick-cooking oats and ½ cup sun-dried cherries to the dry ingredients. Shape and bake the scones as directed above.

Lemon Scones with Fresh Thyme

Omit the poppy seeds and orange zest and add 1 tablespoon grated lemon zest and 2 teaspoons finely chopped fresh thyme to the dry ingredients. Shape and bake the scones as directed above.

Sour Cream Coffee Cake

THE AFFINITY BETWEEN A CUP OF COFFEE AND A LOVELY PIECE OF MOIST CAKE, AT ANY TIME OF THE DAY, NEEDS NO ELABORATION. THIS SOUR CREAM COFFEE CAKE BAKES PERFECTLY WITH OR WITHOUT THE STREUSEL-LIKE FILLING/TOPPING. IF YOU FORGET TO PUT THE FILLING INSIDE, PILE IT ALL ON TOP. THE BATTER CAN ALSO BE USED TO MAKE GREAT MUFFINS WITH THE STREUSEL AS A TOPPING ONLY.

For the streusel filling/topping

4 tablespoons (1/2 stick) cold unsalted butter

1/4 cup packed dark brown sugar

2 tablespoons all-purpose flour

1/4 cup rolled oats

1/2 teaspoon cinnamon

1/2 cup walnuts, coarsely chopped

For the coffee cake

2 1/4 cups all-purpose flour

1 teaspoon baking powder

1/2 teaspoon baking soda

1/2 cup (1 stick) unsalted butter, at room temperature

1 cup sugar

2 large eggs

1 cup sour cream

2 teaspoons vanilla extract

Preheat the oven to 350°F. Grease and flour a 10-inch tube pan.

Prepare the streusel filling/topping: In a small bowl, combine all the streusel ingredients. With your fingertips, rub them together until the mixture is crumbly. Set aside.

Prepare the cake: Sift the flour, baking powder, and baking soda onto a sheet of waxed paper; set aside.

Using the paddle attachment of a standing electric mixer on medium speed, cream the butter until light. Add the sugar and continue to beat until the mixture is light and fluffy. Add the eggs, 1 at a time, beating well after each addition. Add the sour cream and vanilla and continue to beat until blended. Add the dry ingredients and stir until thoroughly combined.

Spoon half of the batter into the prepared tube pan, spreading it with a spatula as evenly as possible. Sprinkle half of the streusel over the batter. Pour the remaining batter into the pan and top it with the remaining streusel, sprinkling it on evenly.

Bake the cake for 45 to 50 minutes, until the edges pull slightly away from the sides of the pan and a skewer inserted in the center of the cake comes out clean. Transfer the cake to a wire rack and let it cool for 20 to 30 minutes before removing it from the pan.

Makes one 10-inch cake

Pear-Anise Coffee Cake

1 ripe pear, such as Anjou, Bartlett, or Bosc

1/2 teaspoon anise seeds

Peel, core, and coarsely chop the pear. Add the pear and anise seeds to the batter after stirring in the dry ingredients. Fill, top, and bake as directed above.

Lemon-Blueberry Coffee Cake

1 cup picked-over fresh or frozen blueberries

Grated zest of 1 large lemon

Omit the streusel filling/topping and stir the blueberries and lemon zest into the batter. Bake as directed above.

Almond Coffee Cake with Dried Cranberries

1/2 cup toasted almonds, coarsely chopped

1/2 cup dried cranberries

1 teaspoon almond extract

Omit the walnuts in the filling/topping mixture and substitute the almonds. Add the cranberries and almond extract to the batter. Fill, top, and bake as directed above.

Hot Couscous Cereal with Honey

BEFORE I FIRST MADE THIS VERY SIMPLE HOT BREAKFAST CEREAL, I COULD NEVER HAVE GUESSED THAT WHEN COOKED WITH MILK, COUSCOUS WOULD HAVE SUCH SWEETNESS AND FLAVOR. THE SESAME SEEDS ADD A LITTLE CRUNCH AND, WITH A CUP OF COFFEE AT BREAKFAST, YOU'RE READY FOR THE DAY. FOR A SPICY VARIATION, STIR IN A TABLESPOON OF DARK BROWN SUGAR AND 1/2 TEASPOON OF CINNAMON.

1 cup milk

1/2 cup couscous, quick-cooking variety

1/2 cup dried blueberries or chopped dried nectarines, peaches, bananas, or any other dried fruit

2 teaspoons sesame seeds

Honey or maple syrup, for serving

In a small saucepan, heat the milk to scalding or until small bubbles form around the edges. Add the couscous, stir once, and cover the pan tightly. Remove the pan from the heat. Let the couscous stand, covered, for 5 minutes.

Stir in the dried fruit and sesame seeds. Divide the couscous between 2 serving bowls and drizzle with honey. Serve at once.

Makes 2 generous servings

Couscous Cereal with Fresh Fruit

Use ¾ cup chopped peeled fresh nectarines or peaches in place of (or as well as) the dried fruit. Serve the cereal as directed above.

Spicy Sweet Potato Soup

· ·

CHILES CHIPOTLE ARE SMOKED JALAPEÑO PEPPERS, USUALLY SOLD CANNED "EN ADOBO," IN TOMATO SAUCE. THE CHILES ARE EXTREMELY HOT AND RICH IN SMOKY FLAVOR. ONE TABLESPOON ADDS THEIR UNIQUE FLAVOR TO THIS SOUP WITHOUT THE "BURN," BUT FEEL FREE TO ADD AS MUCH AS YOU LIKE. SERVE THIS WITH BLACK BEAN, FETA, AND RED SALSA BURRITOS (PAGE 86) FOR A REALLY DELICIOUS DINNER.

1 onion, chopped

3 garlic cloves, minced

4 tablespoons (1/2 stick) unsalted butter

4 sweet potatoes or yams, peeled and chopped into 1 1/2-inch chunks (4 to 5 cups)

8 cups homemade chicken stock or canned chicken broth

1 tablespoon puréed chiles chipotle in adobo sauce (see above)

2 tablespoons fresh lemon juice

Salt and freshly ground black pepper

For garnish

Sour cream

Chopped cilantro

In a 4-quart stockpot or saucepan, sauté the onion and garlic in the butter. Add the sweet potatoes, stir to coat them with the butter, and cook them for 2 to 3 minutes, stirring occasionally. Add the chicken stock and bring it to a boil. Reduce the heat to low and simmer the mixture for 25 minutes, or until the sweet potatoes are soft and completely cooked through.

Strain the soup into a heatproof bowl. Transfer the sweet potatoes to a food processor and purée them, adding just enough of the stock to process them smoothly.

Transfer the sweet potato purée and all the remaining stock to the stockpot, stir to combine, and gently heat through. Add the chipotle purée and lemon juice and season to taste with salt and pepper. Serve the soup in heated soup bowls and garnish each serving with a dollop of sour cream and a sprinkling of chopped cilantro.

Makes 6 to 8 generous servings

Curried Potato and Cauliflower Soup

PAIRED WITH SLICES OF CRUSTY FRESH BREAD, THIS VERY HEARTY THICK SOUP MAKES A LIGHT MEAL IN ITSELF. INCLUDING PEANUT BUTTER MAY SOUND ODD, BUT IN COMBINATION WITH VEGETABLE BROTH, IN PARTICULAR, IT LENDS A RICH, DEEP FLAVOR. FOR MORE VARIETY IN THE TEXTURE, PURÉE ONLY HALF THE VEGETABLES.

2 garlic cloves, minced

1 medium onion, chopped (about 1 cup)

2 stalks celery, chopped (3/4 cup)

4 tablespoons (1/2 stick) unsalted butter

2 tablespoons curry powder

1 tablespoon peanut butter

3 medium potatoes, peeled and coarsely chopped (2 1/2 to 3 cups)

1/2 head cauliflower, cored and coarsely chopped (2 1/2 to 3 cups)

6 cups homemade chicken stock, canned chicken broth, or vegetable broth

2 teaspoons honey

Salt and freshly ground black pepper

In a 4-quart stockpot or saucepan, sauté the garlic, onion, and celery in the butter until the onion is softened and translucent. Add the curry powder and peanut butter and cook for 1 to 2 minutes, stirring often. Add the potatoes and cauliflower, stirring to coat them with the curried spiced butter. Add the chicken stock and bring it to a boil. Reduce the heat to low and simmer the soup for 25 minutes, or until the vegetables are soft and completely cooked through.

Strain the soup into a large heatproof bowl. Transfer the cooked vegetables to a food processor and purée them, a little at a time, adding just enough of the stock to help process them smoothly.

Transfer the vegetable purée and all the remaining stock to the stockpot, stir to combine, and rewarm. Stir in the honey and season with salt and pepper to taste. Serve the soup in heated bowls.

Makes 6 to 8 generous servings

Red Lentil and Corn Chowder

THE LENTIL PURÉE GIVES THIS SOUP ITS CREAMY TEXTURE WITHOUT RENDERING IT HEAVY, WHILE THE THAI SEASONINGS SWEETEN IT SLIGHTLY, CREATING A MILD AND UNUSUAL FLAVOR. IF YOU CAN'T FIND THE SEASONINGS, SUBSTITUTE 1 TEASPOON OF DRIED SAGE OR 2 TEASPOONS OF CHOPPED FRESH SAGE AND 1/4 CUP OF CHOPPED FRESH PARSLEY, WITH A PINCH OF CAYENNE.

1 onion, coarsely chopped

2 garlic cloves, chopped

3 tablespoons olive oil

5 cups red lentils, cooked

6 cups homemade chicken stock, canned chicken broth, or vegetable broth

3 cups fresh or frozen corn, thawed if frozen

1 teaspoon Thai seasonings blend (available in the specialty food section of some markets—a blend of dried lemon grass, galangal, coconut, and ginger)

Salt and freshly ground black pepper

In a 4-quart stockpot or saucepan, sauté the onion and garlic in the olive oil, stirring until the onion is softened and translucent, about 3 to 5 minutes. Add the lentils and enough of the chicken stock to cover the lentils. Bring to a boil and simmer the mixture, partially covered, for 15 to 20 minutes.

Transfer the soup base to a food processor fitted with a metal blade and purée it until smooth. Pour the purée back into the stockpot and add the remaining stock, corn, and Thai seasonings. Season the soup with salt and pepper. Cook over medium heat for 10 to 15 minutes. Serve in heated soup bowls.

Makes 6 to 8 generous servings

Roasted Eggplant and Tomato Soup

MY FRIENDS AT PRANZO ITALIAN GRILL, A FRIENDLY RESTAURANT IN SANTA FE WITH GREAT FOOD, INSPIRED THIS RECIPE. THEY ROAST VEGETABLES LIKE THE ONES HERE AS A BASE FOR SOUPS, STOCKS, AND SAUCES. THIS SOUP IS GREAT SERVED HOT, WITH PARMESAN-COATED CROUTONS, OR CHILLED, WITH A DOLLOP OF SOUR CREAM OR CRÈME FRAÎCHE.

1 eggplant (about 1 pound), ends removed and quartered lengthwise

12 Roma tomatoes, halved lengthwise

8 large garlic cloves

1 red bell pepper, halved and seeded

1 onion, cut into eighths

1/3 cup olive oil

Salt and freshly ground black pepper

6 cups homemade chicken stock or canned chicken broth

2 tablespoons balsamic vinegar

2 teaspoons finely chopped fresh mint

2 teaspoons finely chopped fresh oregano

2 teaspoons chopped fresh thyme

Let the eggplant cool, then scrape the flesh from the skin into a food processor fitted with the metal blade; discard the skin. Add the remaining roasted vegetables to the food processor and purée until smooth. Pour the purée into a large saucepan and stir in the stock, vinegar, and fresh herbs. Heat the soup until it simmers gently. Serve in heated soup bowls.

Makes 6 to 8 servings

Preheat the oven to 450°F.

Place the eggplant, tomatoes, garlic, red bell pepper, and onion in a single layer in a 9 x 12-inch baking dish. Drizzle the olive oil over the vegetables and add salt and pepper to taste. Roast the vegetables, uncovered, for about 30 to 35 minutes, until they are soft and the edges are browned.

NOTE: It is important to use only fresh herbs in this soup. When used in pairs or trios, dried herbs tend to blend together in a muddy, nondescript way, whereas the flavors of fresh herbs remain distinct. If you can't find all three fresh, use just one. If none of these fresh herbs is available, substitute ¼ cup chopped fresh parsley plus 1 to 2 tablespoons fresh lemon juice.

Lemon and Black Pepper Biscotti

. . . .

THE SWEETNESS OF LEMON AND THE SHARPNESS OF FRESHLY-GROUND BLACK PEPPER ARE A REMARKABLY PLEASING COMBINATION. TRY THESE BISCOTTI WITH ROASTED EGGPLANT AND TOMATO SOUP (SEE FACING PAGE), OR SPREAD THEM WITH GOAT CHEESE, TOP WITH DICED TOMATOES, AND SERVE AS AN APPETIZER WITH A GLASS OF WINE.

2 cups all-purpose flour

1/4 cup freshly grated Parmesan cheese

1/2 cup almonds, finely ground

1 1/2 teaspoons baking powder

Grated zest of 1 lemon

1 1/2 teaspoons fresh coarse ground
black pepper

1/2 cup (1 stick) unsalted butter,
at room temperature

2 tablespoons sugar

2 large eggs

Preheat the oven to 375°F. Grease a baking sheet.

In a bowl, combine the flour, cheese, almonds, baking powder, zest, and black pepper; set aside.

Using the paddle attachment of a standing electric mixer on medium speed, cream the butter until light. Add the sugar and continue to beat until the mixture is light and creamy. Add the eggs, 1 at a time, and beat until smooth. Add the dry ingredients and mix until combined.

On a lightly floured work surface, divide the dough into 2 parts. Roll each half into a log about 2 inches in diameter. Transfer the logs to the prepared baking sheet, leaving several inches in between, and bake them for about 20 minutes, until the edges are lightly browned and the centers are almost firm to the touch. Remove from the oven and let the logs cool on the baking sheet for 10 to 15 minutes.

With a serrated knife, cut each log on the diagonal into slices about 1 inch thick. Return the biscotti, cut side down, to the baking sheet and bake them for about 10 minutes, until the edges are lightly browned. Transfer the biscotti to a wire rack to cool. Store in an airtight container.

*Makes about twenty-four
2 1/2-inch biscotti*

Pasta e Fagioli

USE ALMOST ANY COMBINATION OF COOKED BEANS BUT THERE SHOULD ALWAYS BE MORE BEANS AND VEGETABLES THAN LIQUID IN THIS HEARTY, THICK SOUP/STEW. WITH ONION, PARMESAN, AND PROSCIUTTO MUFFINS (PAGE 90) AND ESPRESSO GRANITA (PAGE 140) AS A COOLING CONCLUSION, IT IS A MEAL IN ITSELF.

1/2 cup olive oil

3 garlic cloves, minced

1 onion, chopped

3 stalks celery, chopped

3 carrots, peeled and chopped

2 medium zucchini, cut lengthwise in half and sliced crosswise

1/2 pound green beans, cut into 2-inch pieces

One 28-ounce can whole tomatoes, with juice

8 to **10** cups homemade chicken stock or canned chicken broth

One 15-ounce can red kidney beans, drained and rinsed

One 15-ounce can small white beans, drained and rinsed

One 15-ounce can fava beans, drained and rinsed

5 to **6** sun-dried tomatoes packed in oil, drained and finely chopped

3 tablespoons chopped fresh basil

2 teaspoons finely chopped fresh thyme

Salt and freshly ground black pepper

1/2 pound small pasta, such as bows, macaroni, twists, or small shells, cooked and drained

Freshly grated Parmesan cheese, for garnish

In a medium-size stockpot, heat the olive oil until hot. Add the garlic, onion, celery, and carrots and sauté until all the vegetables are softened and the onion is translucent. Add the zucchini and green beans and cook, stirring, for several minutes more. Add the tomatoes with their juice, the chicken stock, canned beans, and sun-dried tomatoes and bring the mixture to a boil. Reduce the heat to low and simmer the soup for 30 to 45 minutes, stirring occasionally, until the vegetables are cooked through. Add the basil and thyme and season with salt and pepper to taste.

Just before serving, stir in the cooked pasta and heat until it is heated through. Ladle the soup into heated serving bowls and garnish each serving with Parmesan cheese.

Makes 8 to 10 generous servings

Fresh Mozzarella and
Salsa Sandwich

· ·

THE CLASSIC ITALIAN FIRST COURSE OF CREAMY, MILD FRESH MOZZARELLA, RIPE TOMATOES, AND FRAGRANT BASIL LEAVES TURNS UP HERE BETWEEN SLICES OF WHOLE-GRAIN BREAD MOISTENED WITH A CHUNKY ROASTED BELL PEPPER SALSA. THIS SANDWICH IS BEST MADE JUST BEFORE SERVING.

1 red bell pepper

1 green bell pepper

3 thin slices red onion

1 garlic clove, finely chopped

3 tablespoons olive oil

1 tablespoon fresh lemon juice

1 tablespoon red wine vinegar or balsamic vinegar

Salt and freshly ground black pepper

8 slices whole-grain bread

3 to **4** balls (4 ounces each) fresh mozzarella, sliced 1/4 inch thick

3 to **4** tomatoes, sliced (about 16 slices)

12 to **16** whole basil leaves

Roast the bell peppers over a gas flame: Light the gas burner, then put the peppers directly on the burner. As the skin of each pepper becomes blistered and charred, but before it turns black, turn the pepper with metal tongs. When the entire skin of each pepper is roasted, wrap the peppers loosely in paper towels and place in a plastic bag.

Seal the bag and let the peppers steam for 10 to 15 minutes. Remove the peppers from the bag and towels and peel off the charred skin. Halve the peppers, core and seed them, and chop the flesh coarsely.

In a bowl, combine the roasted peppers with the onion, garlic, olive oil, lemon juice, and vinegar. Season the salsa to taste with salt and pepper.

Assemble the sandwiches: Spread 2 tablespoons of the salsa on each of 4 slices of the bread. Top the salsa with the fresh mozzarella slices, tomato slices, and basil leaves, dividing them equally. Spread the remaining bread with additional salsa and place on top. Cut the sandwiches into quarters, arrange on plates, and serve.

Makes 4 sandwiches

Grilled Chicken Sandwich with Blue Cheese Spread

I LIKE THIS SANDWICH BEST WHEN IT IS MADE WITH GRILLED CHICKEN, BUT ANY CHICKEN WILL DO—EVEN GOOD-QUALITY SLICED SMOKED CHICKEN BREAST. TOAST THE WALNUTS ON A BAKING SHEET IN A PREHEATED 375°F. OVEN FOR ABOUT 15 MINUTES, OR IN A DRY SKILLET OVER MEDIUM-HIGH HEAT, STIRRING THEM OFTEN, UNTIL THE EDGES ARE BROWNED. LET COOL BEFORE CHOPPING AND MIXING THEM WITH THE CHEESE.

For the blue cheese and walnut spread

4 to **5** ounces creamy blue cheese, such as blue Chantal, bleu de Bresse, or Gorgonzola

1/2 cup walnuts, toasted (see above) and chopped medium-fine

1/4 cup chopped fresh parsley

1 tablespoon sherry vinegar

8 slices whole-grain or other bread, toasted

4 cooked boneless skinless chicken breasts, preferably grilled or sautéed

20 thin slices cucumber

Prepare the blue cheese and walnut spread: In a small bowl, using the back of a wooden spoon, gently mash the blue cheese, walnuts, parsley, and vinegar together until combined but still chunky.

Spread each slice of toast with about 1 tablespoon of the cheese and walnut spread. Place 1 chicken breast on each of 4 pieces of the toast and top with 5 slices of cucumber. Top with the remaining toast. Arrange on plates, and serve at once.

Makes 4 sandwiches

Curried Eggplant, Chutney, and Watercress Sandwich

· ·

HERE'S AN INTERESTINGLY OFFBEAT ALTERNATIVE TO THE STANDARD MEAT AND CHEESE SANDWICH COMBINATIONS. THE EGGPLANT IS DIPPED FIRST INTO EGG, THEN INTO SPICED CORNMEAL, AND SAUTÉED. USE CRUSTY FRENCH ROLLS OR SOFT SEMOLINA BREAD. IF WATERCRESS IS UNAVAILABLE, SUBSTITUTE ANOTHER PEPPERY GREEN, SUCH AS ARUGULA.

2 large eggs

1 cup yellow cornmeal

1 tablespoon plus **1** teaspoon curry powder

1/2 teaspoon salt

1/4 teaspoon freshly ground black pepper

1/2 teaspoon red pepper flakes (optional)

1/4 to **1/2** cup olive oil

1 small eggplant (about 12 ounces), sliced lengthwise into 1/4-inch-thick slices and trimmed to fit the rolls

4 large French rolls, halved horizontally

1/2 cup mango chutney, such as Major Grey's

1 bunch watercress, rinsed, dried, and coarse stem ends removed

Preheat the oven to 250°F.

In a shallow bowl, beat the eggs lightly with a fork. In another shallow bowl or pie plate, combine the cornmeal, curry powder, salt, black pepper, and red pepper flakes, if using.

Heat 3 tablespoons of the olive oil in a large sauté pan or heavy skillet. Dip the egg-plant, a slice at a time, into the egg, making sure both sides are moistened, then dredge it in the spiced cornmeal, coating both sides completely. Add the breaded eggplant slices to the pan, arranging them in a single layer, and cook over medium heat for 2 to 3 minutes, turning them to brown both sides, until the eggplant is tender when tested with a fork. Transfer the eggplant slices to paper towels to drain, then keep them warm on a baking sheet in the preheated oven while you dip and sauté the remaining eggplant slices in the same manner.

Spread both sides of the rolls with 1 tablespoon each of the chutney. Top each bottom half with slices of the warm eggplant and cover with watercress sprigs. Top with the remaining halves. Serve immediately, while the eggplant is still warm.

Makes 4 sandwiches

Sweet and Spicy
Couscous Salad

ALTHOUGH COUSCOUS IS TRADITIONALLY STEAMED IN A SPECIAL SIEVE-LIKE CONTAINER OVER A BUBBLING SPICY MOROCCAN STEW CALLED A TAGINE, I USE THE QUICK-COOKING VARIETY, PREPARED IN A SAUCEPAN. TOASTING THE CUMIN SEEDS FOR THE VINAIGRETTE ADDS A MORE AROMATIC AND NUTTIER FLAVOR TO THE SALAD.

For the salad

3 cups couscous, quick-cooking variety, cooked and cooled

1 cup diced zucchini

1 cup coarsely grated carrots

1/2 cup thinly sliced red onion

1 red, yellow, or green bell pepper, seeded and diced

1/2 cup finely chopped fresh parsley

1/2 cup raisins

1 cup cooked, drained chick-peas (optional)

For the orange vinaigrette

1 1/2 teaspoons cumin seeds, toasted (see Note)

1/3 cup orange juice

2 tablespoons fresh lemon juice

1 tablespoon honey

1/2 teaspoon cinnamon

Pinch of cayenne pepper (optional)

1/2 cup olive oil

1 tablespoon walnut oil (optional)

Salt and freshly ground black pepper

Prepare the salad: In a large bowl, combine the cooked couscous, zucchini, carrots, red onion, bell pepper, parsley, raisins, and chick-peas, if desired.

Prepare the orange vinaigrette: In a small bowl, whisk together the cumin seeds, orange juice, lemon juice, honey, cinnamon, and cayenne, if desired. Add the olive oil and walnut oil, if desired, in a slow steady stream, whisking until combined.

Pour the dressing over the couscous salad and toss well to combine. Season the salad with salt and pepper to taste. Serve immediately or refrigerate, covered, for up to 24 hours.

Makes 6 to 8 servings

NOTE: To toast cumin seeds, place the seeds in a small sauté pan over medium heat, and stir occasionally until they start to brown. Remove from the heat.

Pasta Salad with Tomato Vinaigrette

. . . .

THIS SALAD IS BRIGHT WITH COLOR AND FLAVOR, ESPECIALLY WHEN MADE WITH A GOOD WINE VINEGAR AND EXTRA-VIRGIN OLIVE OIL. YOU CAN PREPARE IT THE DAY BEFORE A PARTY OR PICNIC, BUT KEEP THE DRESSING SEPARATE FROM THE PASTA AND VEGETABLES: TOSS EVERYTHING TOGETHER AN HOUR OR TWO BEFORE SERVING. LEMON BUTTER TWISTS (PAGE 117) AND TALL ICED COFFEES WOULD ROUND OUT AN EASY SUMMER BUFFET.

For the pasta salad

12 ounces short pasta, such as wheels, twists, macaroni, or penne, cooked and drained

One 8-ounce can artichoke hearts, drained and quartered

5 ounces feta cheese, crumbled

2 small yellow squash, cut in half length-wise and sliced crosswise 1/4 inch thick

1 red bell pepper, seeded and julienned

1 green bell pepper, seeded and julienned

1 red onion, thinly sliced

1 cup black olives, Kalamata or Niçoise, pitted

1 cup fresh fennel slivers (cut lengthwise 1/4 inch thick)

3/4 cup finely chopped fresh parsley

1/2 cup coarsely chopped fresh basil

For the tomato vinaigrette

4 Roma tomatoes, coarsely chopped

2 sun-dried tomatoes packed in oil, drained and finely chopped

1/3 cup white wine vinegar

2 tablespoons fresh lemon juice

2/3 cup olive oil, preferably extra virgin

Salt and freshly ground black pepper

Prepare the pasta salad: In a large bowl, toss together all the salad ingredients.

Prepare the tomato vinaigrette: In a small bowl, whisk together all the vinai-grette ingredients, except the olive oil. Add the oil in a slow steady stream, whisking until combined.

Pour the dressing over the pasta salad and toss gently. Add salt and pepper to taste.

Makes 6 generous servings

Summer Rice Salad
with Pine Nuts

TRY TO FIND BASMATI OR TEXMATI RICE TO MAKE THIS SALAD. EACH WILL LEND AN INTERESTING POPCORN-TYPE FLAVOR AND CHEWY TEXTURE. FOR AN EASY BUT ELEGANT DINNER: SERVE GRILLED CHICKEN BREASTS, THIS SALAD, CRUSTY FRENCH BREAD, AND CHOCOLATE-MINT POTS DE CRÈME (PAGE 138).

For the dressing

1 tablespoon Dijon mustard

3 tablespoons white wine vinegar or tarragon vinegar

1 tablespoon fresh lemon juice

1/3 cup olive oil

For the salad

2 cups cooked Basmati, Texmati, or other long-grained white rice

1 cup frozen peas, thawed

1 cup snow peas, strings removed and blanched (optional)

1/2 cup paper-thin slices red onion

1/2 cup finely chopped fresh parsley

1/4 cup pine nuts, toasted

2 tablespoons chopped fresh dill or **1** tablespoon dried dill

1 tablespoon capers (optional)

1 tablespoon finely chopped fresh thyme

Salt and freshly ground black pepper

Prepare the dressing: In a large salad bowl, whisk together the mustard, vinegar, and lemon juice. Add the olive oil in a slow steady stream, whisking until combined.

Prepare the salad: Add all the salad ingredients to the salad bowl and toss well to combine. Add salt and pepper to taste. Serve the salad at room temperature or chilled.

Makes 4 to 6 servings

Rice Salad
with Asparagus

Substitute 2 cups chopped asparagus, blanched, for the snow peas, ½ cup chopped scallions for the red onion, and toasted slivered almonds for the pine nuts.

Crab-Stuffed French Toast

MADE WITH THICK-SLICED CHALLAH, COARSE WHOLE-GRAIN, OR A PEASANT LOAF, FRENCH TOAST ADDS ANOTHER DIMENSION TO SANDWICH-MAKING. THE CRAB FILLING MAKES THIS VERSION FANCY ENOUGH TO SERVE FOR BRUNCH OR SUNDAY SUPPER. CUT THE SANDWICHES INTO FINGERS TO MAKE AN EASY HORS D'OEUVRE, BUT ASSEMBLE AHEAD OF TIME IF YOU ARE HAVING A CROWD.

For the crab filling

- **8** ounces cream cheese, softened
- **4 1/2** ounces fresh or canned crabmeat, picked over
- **1** tablespoon finely chopped fresh parsley
- **2** teaspoons finely chopped fresh dill
- **2** teaspoons fresh lemon juice

- **8** thick slices challah, whole-grain, or peasant bread
- **3** large eggs
- **3** tablespoons milk
- **3** to **4** tablespoons unsalted butter, or more as needed

Prepare the crab filling: In a bowl, stir together all the filling ingredients until a smooth paste is formed.

Spread 1 quarter of the crab filling on each of 4 slices of the bread. Top with the remaining slices. In a wide shallow bowl, whisk together the eggs and milk.

Heat a griddle or a heavy-bottomed skillet until hot. Grease the cooking surface with 1 to 2 tablespoons butter. Dip each sandwich into the egg mixture, coating both sides. Place the sandwiches in the hot pan or griddle and cook for 2 to 3 minutes, until golden brown. Add more butter if necessary before turning the sandwiches over and cooking them until golden brown. Remove each French toast sandwich to a plate, cut it into quarters, and serve at once.

Makes 4 servings

Southwest Burgers

CHOPPED GREEN OLIVES AND RED CHILE KETCHUP ARE JUST WHAT'S NEEDED TO PERK UP A BURGER. PURE GROUND NEW MEXICAN RED CHILE, AVAILABLE AT SOME GOURMET FOOD STORES, ADDS SPICE TO A TRADITIONAL BARBECUE SAUCE THAT INCLUDES A HEADY AMOUNT OF COFFEE. YOU CAN DOUBLE THE CHILE KETCHUP RECIPE TO USE AS A DIPPING SAUCE FOR CHICKEN WINGS OR COLD SHRIMP.

For the Red Chile Ketchup (Makes 3/4 cup)

1 tablespoon olive oil

1/2 onion, coarsely chopped

2 garlic cloves, finely chopped

1/2 teaspoon ground cumin or **1/4** teaspoon cumin seeds

1/4 cup pure ground New Mexican red chile (see above) or **2** tablespoons chili powder

1/2 cup black coffee

1/3 cup tomato ketchup

Salt and freshly ground black pepper

For the burgers

1 1/2 pounds ground beef

1/4 cup coarsely chopped green olives

1 tablespoon Dijon mustard

4 oat or other whole-grain hamburger buns, halved horizontally

4 slices Monterey Jack cheese (optional)

Prepare the Red Chile Ketchup: In a small sauté pan, heat the olive oil until hot. Add the onion and garlic and cook over medium heat until the onion is translucent and soft. Add the cumin and ground chile, stirring constantly to make a paste. Add the coffee and stir until smooth. Add the ketchup and stir to combine. Reduce the heat to low and simmer the mixture for 2 to 3 minutes.

Transfer the mixture to a food processor fitted with the metal blade and process until smooth. Season to taste with salt and pepper. The ketchup may be used warm, at room temperature, or chilled.

Preheat the broiler.

Prepare the burgers: In a bowl, combine the beef, olives, and mustard. Form the mixture into 4 equal patties.

Broil the burgers about 6 inches from the heat for 5 to 7 minutes on each side, or until completely cooked through.

While the burgers cook, lightly toast the hamburger buns.

Place a burger on the bottom half of each toasted bun, top the burger with a slice of cheese, if desired, and spoon a tablespoon or two of the Red Chile Ketchup over the top. Top with the remaining buns and serve immediately. If desired, serve additional Red Chile Ketchup as an accompaniment.

Makes 4 servings

Southwest Turkey Meat Loaf

3 pounds ground turkey

1 recipe Red Chile Ketchup (opposite page)

1 1/2 cups bread crumbs

2 large eggs

1/4 cup chopped green olives (optional)

1/2 cup chopped fresh parsley

1 tablespoon Dijon mustard

1 medium onion, coarsely chopped

Salt and freshly ground black pepper
   to taste

Preheat the oven to 350°F.

In a bowl, mix all the meat loaf ingredients together until well combined. Turn into an 8 x 5 x 3-inch loaf pan, packing firmly into a loaf shape. Bake for 1 hour.

Makes 6 to 8 servings

Brownies

IF YOU DON'T HAVE TIME TO MAKE A CAKE, TRY BROWNIES. THEY ARE EASY TO PUT TOGETHER, AND YOU DON'T EVEN NEED AN ELECTRIC MIXER. THE VARIATIONS ARE ENDLESS, AND WHEN DRESSED UP WITH ICE CREAM AND A CHOCOLATE SAUCE (PAGE 142), BROWNIES BECOME FANCY ENOUGH FOR A PARTY.

1 1/2 cups all-purpose flour

1/2 teaspoon baking powder

1/2 teaspoon salt

1 cup (2 sticks) unsalted butter, cut into pieces

4 ounces unsweetened chocolate, coarsely chopped

1 tablespoon instant coffee

1 3/4 cups sugar

4 large eggs

2 teaspoons vanilla extract

Preheat the oven to 350°F. Grease and flour a 9-inch square baking pan.

Into a bowl, sift together the flour, baking powder, and salt; set aside.

In the top of a double boiler set over gently simmering water, melt the butter and chocolate with the instant coffee, stirring until smooth. Pour the butter-chocolate mixture into a bowl, add the sugar, and stir until it is incorporated. Add the eggs, 1 at a time, beating well after each addition. Stir in the vanilla. Stir in the dry ingredients until the batter is smooth. Do not overmix.

Spread the batter evenly in the prepared pan and bake for 22 to 25 minutes, or until the brownies are just set. (The center of the brownies should still be wet when tested with a skewer.) Let the brownies cool on a wire rack before cutting them into squares.

Makes sixteen 2 1/4-inch squares

Currant and Walnut Biscotti

BISCOTTI ARE TWICE-BAKED HARD ITALIAN COOKIES, TRADITIONALLY ENJOYED DIPPED INTO VIN SANTO. THESE BISCOTTI ARE NEITHER AS LONG NOR AS DRY AS THE ONES I SOMETIMES HAVE IN CAFÉS. I LIKE THEM ANYTIME DURING THE DAY, INCLUDING AT BREAKFAST. NOT TOO SWEET, THEY TEND TO MELLOW THE INTENSITY OF ESPRESSO.

2 1/2 cups all-purpose flour

1 teaspoon baking powder

1/2 cup walnuts, finely chopped

1/4 cup dried currants

1/2 cup (1 stick) unsalted butter, at room temperature

3/4 cup sugar

2 large eggs

1 tablespoon vanilla extract, brandy, or Marsala

Preheat the oven to 350°F. Grease a baking sheet.

In a bowl, stir together the flour, baking powder, walnuts, and currants; set aside.

Using the paddle attachment of a standing electric mixer on medium speed, cream the butter until light. Add the sugar and continue to beat until the mixture is light and fluffy. Add the eggs, 1 at a time, and beat until smooth. Beat in the vanilla. Stir in the dry ingredients until the dough is well combined.

On a floured work surface, divide the dough into 2 parts. Roll each half into a log 12 to 14 inches long. Transfer the logs to the prepared baking sheet, leaving several inches between them. Bake them about 20 minutes, until the edges are browned and the centers are almost firm to the touch. Remove the baking sheet from the oven and let the baked logs cool on the baking sheet for 15 to 20 minutes.

With a serrated knife, cut each log on the diagonal into slices about ¾ inch thick. Return the biscotti, cut sides down, to the baking sheet and bake them about 8 to 10 minutes, until the edges look toasted. Transfer the biscotti to a wire rack to cool. Store in an airtight container.

Makes about twenty-four 2 1/2-inch cookies

Chocolate-Dipped
Almond Biscotti

GROUND ANISE OR ANISESEED IS THE TRADITIONAL FLAVORING FOR PLAIN BISCOTTI. IN

THESE CHOCOLATE-DIPPED BISCOTTI, A SCANT 1/4 TEASPOON WOULD BE DELICIOUS. OR,

YOU CAN ADD THE SPICE OF YOUR CHOICE: CINNAMON, A PINCH OF CLOVES, OR NUTMEG.

2 1/4 cups all-purpose flour

1/2 cup unsweetened cocoa, preferably
Dutch process

1/2 cup almonds, finely ground

1 3/4 teaspoons baking powder

1/2 cup (1 stick) unsalted butter, at room
temperature

2/3 cup sugar

2 large eggs

1 tablespoon amaretto

2 teaspoons instant coffee dissolved in
1 tablespoon hot coffee

6 ounces semisweet chocolate, melted,
for dipping

Preheat the oven to 375°F. Grease a baking sheet.

In a bowl, combine the flour, cocoa, almonds, and baking powder; set aside.

Using the paddle attachment of a standing electric mixer on medium speed, cream the butter until light. Add the sugar and continue to beat until the mixture is light and creamy. Add the eggs, 1 at a time, and

beat until smooth. Stir in the amaretto and coffee. Add the dry ingredients and stir until thoroughly combined.

Form the dough into logs as directed on page 113. Bake for 20 to 25 minutes, until the centers are almost firm to the touch. Cool, cut, and bake a second time as directed on page 113. Cool on a wire rack.

Dip 1 end of each biscotti into the melted chocolate, letting the excess drip back into the bowl, and place the biscotti on a piece of waxed paper or parchment paper to let the chocolate set.

*Makes about twenty-four
2 1/2-inch cookies*

Coconut Chocolate Chip Cookies

EVERYONE HAS A FAVORITE CHOCOLATE CHIP COOKIE RECIPE. THESE HAVE A SLIGHT COCONUT FLAVOR AND SOFT, CHEWY TEXTURE. THE COFFEE IN THEM IS VERY SUBTLE. I ESPECIALLY LIKE THESE WITH ESPRESSO MACCHIATO (PAGE 78) OR LATTE MACCHIATO (PAGE 79). OR SERVE THEM FOR DESSERT, CRUMBLED OVER A LUSCIOUS ICE CREAM.

2 1/4 cups all-purpose flour

1 teaspoon baking soda

1/4 teaspoon salt

1 cup unsalted butter (2 sticks), at room temperature

1 cup firmly packed light brown sugar

3/4 cup granulated sugar

2 large eggs

2 teaspoons instant coffee dissolved in 1 tablespoon hot coffee

1 1/2 cups semisweet chocolate chips

1/2 cup sweetened or unsweetened shredded coconut

Preheat the oven to 350°F. Grease 2 baking sheets.

Into a bowl, sift together the flour, baking soda, and salt; set aside.

Using the paddle attachment of a standing electric mixer on medium speed, cream the butter and the brown and granulated sugars until light and creamy. Add the eggs and coffee and beat until well combined. Add the sifted dry ingredients and stir to combine. Stir in the chocolate chips and coconut until thoroughly incorporated.

Drop the dough by tablespoonfuls onto the prepared baking sheets, leaving 1½ inches between each cookie. Bake the cookies for 10 to 12 minutes, until golden brown around the edges but still soft in the center. Transfer the cookies to a wire rack to cool completely. Store the cookies in layers in airtight containers.

Makes thirty-six 3 1/2-inch cookies

Mocha Spice Butter Cookies

ALTHOUGH CAYENNE PEPPER IS NOT USUALLY AN INGREDIENT IN BUTTER COOKIE RECIPES,
IT LENDS A SLIGHT BUT PLEASANT BITE TO THESE BITTERSWEET CHOCOLATEY COOKIES. FOR
A FANCIER LOOK, DRIZZLE MELTED WHITE CHOCOLATE FROM A FORK OVER THE COOKIES
ONCE THEY HAVE COOLED. THEY'RE A NATURAL PARTNER WITH HOT, OR EVEN ICED, COFFEE.

1 1/2 cups all-purpose flour

3/4 cup unsweetened cocoa, preferably Dutch process

1/2 teaspoon cinnamon

1/4 teaspoon cayenne pepper

1 cup (2 sticks) unsalted butter, at room temperature

1 cup sugar

1 large egg

1 tablespoon instant coffee dissolved in 1 tablespoon hot coffee or espresso

2 teaspoons vanilla extract

Preheat the oven to 375°F. Generously grease 2 baking sheets.

Sift together the flour, cocoa, cinnamon, and cayenne onto a sheet of waxed paper; set aside.

Using the paddle attachment of a standing electric mixer on medium speed, cream the butter and sugar until light and fluffy. Add the egg, coffee, and vanilla and mix until well combined. Add the reserved sifted dry ingredients and stir until the dough forms a ball. Turn the dough out onto a lightly floured surface and knead it several times. Wrap the dough in plastic wrap or waxed paper and chill it for at least 30 minutes.

Divide the chilled dough in half. Roll one half of it out on a lightly floured surface until it is about ¼ inch thick. With a small (2-inch) cookie cutter, cut out shapes and arrange them on one of the prepared baking sheets. Bake the cookies for 5 to 8 minutes. (The cookies should be removed from the oven while they are still soft in the center. They will crisp as they cool.) Transfer to a wire rack to cool.

Roll out the remaining dough, cut out cookies, bake, and cool in the same manner.

Store the cookies in layers in airtight containers.

Makes about forty 2-inch cookies

Lemon Butter Twists

. . . .

IF YOU LIKE ESPRESSO ROMANO—THAT IS, ESPRESSO WITH A LEMON TWIST—THIS IS THE
COOKIE TO HAVE WITH IT. THE DOUGH CAN ALSO BE ROLLED OUT, THEN CUT WITH COOKIE
CUTTERS OR, LIKE REFRIGERATOR COOKIE DOUGH, SIMPLY SLICED INTO ROUNDS. FOR THE
HOLIDAYS, DRESS UP THESE TWISTS BY ROLLING THE DOUGH IN CHOPPED PISTACHIO NUTS.

3/4 cup unsalted butter (1 1/2 sticks),
softened

1 cup sugar

1/2 teaspoon almond extract

2 large eggs

Grated zest of 1 lemon

2 1/2 cups all-purpose flour

Preheat the oven to 350°F. Grease 2 baking sheets.

Using a standing electric mixer fitted with the paddle attachment, cream the butter and sugar until light and fluffy. Add the almond extract, eggs, and lemon zest, mixing well. Add the flour and mix thoroughly until a dough forms.

Divide the dough in half. Roll each half on a floured surface into a cylinder about 2 inches in diameter. Refrigerate one cylinder of dough. Cut the remaining cylinder into ½-inch slices. On a lightly floured work surface, roll each slice into a rope 6 inches long. Fold the rope in half and twist it to form a 3-inch twist. (You may need to refrigerate the dough if it becomes too sticky to work with.) Place the twists on 1 of the prepared baking sheets, about 1 inch apart. Bake 9 to 12 minutes, until the edges start to turn golden. Transfer the cookies to wire racks to cool.

Repeat with remaining cylinder.

Store the cookies in layers in an airtight container.

Makes forty 3-inch cookies

Oat Shortbread

THIS VARIATION ON TRADITIONAL BUTTER-RICH SHORTBREAD HAS A NUTTY OAT FLAVOR
AND SOMEWHAT CRUNCHY TEXTURE. I LIKE A WEDGE WITH AN ORANGE- OR HAZELNUT-
FLAVORED LATTE OR AN ESPRESSO IN THE LATE AFTERNOON WITH THE DAY'S NEWS.
BE SURE TO USE THE OLD-FASHIONED TYPE OF ROLLED OATS RATHER THAN THE QUICK-
COOKING VARIETY TO GET THE RIGHT CHEWY TEXTURE.

2/3 cup all-purpose flour

3/4 cup rolled oats

2 tablespoons cornstarch

1/2 cup (1 stick) unsalted butter, at room
temperature

1/3 cup firmly packed light brown sugar

1 teaspoon vanilla extract

Preheat the oven to 325°F. Lightly grease a 9-inch pie plate.

In a bowl, combine the flour, oats, and cornstarch; set aside.

Using the paddle attachment of a standing electric mixer on medium, cream the butter until light and fluffy. Add the brown sugar and beat until well incorporated. Stir in the vanilla. Add the dry ingredients and mix until well blended.

Pat the shortbread dough evenly over the bottom of the prepared pie plate. Place the plate in the freezer for 10 minutes, until the dough is firm to the touch. Prick the dough all over with the tines of a fork.

Bake the shortbread for 30 to 35 minutes, until the edges are barely beginning to brown; the center will still be quite soft. Remove the pie plate from the oven and let it stand for 10 to 15 minutes on a wire rack. With a sharp knife, score the shortbread into 12 to 16 wedges. Let the wedges cool in the plate before removing them with a spatula. Store in an airtight container at room temperature.

Makes 12 to 16 wedges

Madeleines au Chocolat

FAMOUS FOR THEIR SIMPLICITY AND DELICATE SHELL SHAPE, MADELEINES ARE THE PERFECT ACCOMPANIMENT TO A STEAMING CUP OF COFFEE, AND ARE AT THEIR BEST SERVED ON THE DAY THEY ARE MADE. THOUGH MADELEINES ARE USUALLY FLAVORED WITH LEMON ZEST, THIS DELICIOUS VARIATION IS ENRICHED WITH COCOA AND SPIKED WITH COFFEE. YOU WILL NEED A MADELEINE PAN, AVAILABLE AT ANY GOOD HOUSEWARES STORE.

3/4 cup all-purpose flour

1/2 unsweetened cocoa powder, preferably Dutch process

2 large eggs

1 large egg yolk

2 teaspoons instant coffee dissolved in 1 tablespoon hot coffee

3/4 cup confectioners' sugar, plus additional for dusting (optional)

1/2 cup (1 stick) unsalted butter, melted and cooled

Preheat the oven to 350°F. Carefully grease and then flour the shell-shaped molds of 2 madeleine pans.

Sift the flour and cocoa together twice onto a sheet of waxed paper; set aside.

Using the whip attachment of an electric mixer on high speed, beat the eggs and egg yolk until thick and light, 3 to 4 minutes. Whip in the coffee. Gradually add the ¾ cup confectioners' sugar and continue to whip until the mixture is thick and light and falls in a ribbon when the beater is lifted. Using a rubber spatula, fold in the dry ingredients. Fold in the melted butter quickly and gently until thoroughly incorporated.

Spoon the batter into the prepared madeleine molds, filling them completely. Use a knife or small metal spatula to spread the batter evenly if necessary. Bake for 10 to 12 minutes, or until the madeleines spring back when touched lightly with your fingertip. Let the madeleines stand in the pans a minute or 2 before turning them out to cool on a wire rack. Dust with confectioners' sugar before serving, if desired.

Makes eighteen 3-inch cakes

Blueberry and Buttermilk Pie

THIS IS AN OLD-FASHIONED COMFORT PIE. THE FILLING IS SMOOTH AND SWEET, LIGHT AND REFRESHING. I LIKE THE CONTRAST OF CHEWY BERRIES WITH THE SILKINESS OF THE CUSTARD, ESPECIALLY IN THE LATE AFTERNOON WITH A CUP OF BLACK COFFEE. IF DRIED BLUEBERRIES ARE NOT AVAILABLE, DRIED CHERRIES OR CRANBERRIES OR ALMOST ANY DRIED FRUIT CAN BE SUBSTITUTED.

For the crust

1 1/4 cups all-purpose flour

2 tablespoons sugar

1/2 cup (1 stick) cold unsalted butter, cut into teaspoon-sized pieces

3 to **4** tablespoons cold water

For the filling

3 large eggs

1 cup sugar

2/3 cup dried blueberries

2 tablespoons all-purpose flour

Grated zest of 1 lemon

1 cup buttermilk

4 tablespoons (1/2 stick) unsalted butter, melted

1/2 teaspoon almond extract

Prepare the crust: In a bowl, combine the flour and sugar. Using 2 knives, a pastry blender, or your fingertips, work the butter into the flour mixture until it is crumbly and resembles cornmeal. Add the cold water, a tablespoon at a time, stirring just until the dough comes together into a ball.

Turn the dough out onto a lightly floured work surface and knead it once or twice. If the dough is too sticky to roll out, wrap it in plastic wrap and chill it until firm.

On a lightly floured work surface roll the dough into an 11-inch round. Fit the dough carefully into a 9-inch pie plate and crimp the edges decoratively. With the tines of a fork, prick the dough in several places. Chill the shell while you prepare the filling.

Preheat the oven to 400°F.

Prepare the filling: Using a handheld electric mixer on high speed, beat the eggs until slightly thickened. Gradually add the sugar and continue to beat until the mixture is thick and light.

Pasta Salad with
Tomato Vinaigrette
(PAGE 107)

Spicy Sweet
Potato Soup
(PAGE 97)

Assorted Relishes
and Pickles

Grilled Chicken
Sandwich with Blue
Cheese Spread
(PAGE 104)

Crusty Bread

Blueberry and
Buttermilk Pie

Almond Tart
(PAGE 122)

Any Good Black
Coffee

Espresso Lungo
(PAGE 78)

In a bowl, toss the dried blueberries with 1 tablespoon of the flour; set aside.

Add the remaining tablespoon of flour and lemon zest to the egg and sugar mixture, and beat. Gradually add the buttermilk and continue to beat until the buttermilk is incorporated. Add the melted butter and almond extract. Stir in the blueberries.

Pour the filling into the prepared pie shell and bake the pie for 10 minutes.

Reduce the oven temperature to 350°F and continue to bake the pie until the filling is set and a skewer inserted in the center of the filling comes out clean, about 25 to 30 minutes. Transfer the pie to a wire rack and let it cool completely. Then refrigerate it until thoroughly chilled. Serve chilled.

Makes one 9-inch pie, 8 servings

Almond Tart

PAIRED WITH A CUP OF GOOD BLACK COFFEE, ALMOND TART, IN ANY OF ITS MANY VARIATIONS, IS ONE OF MY FAVORITE DESSERTS. THIS RECIPE IS NOT AS SWEET AS MANY VERSIONS AND RELIES LESS ON THE SOMETIMES OVERPOWERING TASTE OF ALMOND PASTE. I USE UNTOASTED ALMONDS HERE, BUT YOU CAN TOAST THEM TO ADD A WONDERFUL ROASTED FLAVOR TO THE FILLING.

For the crust

1 1/4 cups all-purpose flour

2 tablespoons sugar

1/2 cup (1 stick) cold unsalted butter, cut into teaspoon-sized pieces

4 to **5** tablespoons cold water

For the almond filling

4 tablespoons (1/2 stick) butter, at room temperature

3/4 cup sugar

3 1/2 ounces almond paste

2 large eggs

2 tablespoons all-purpose flour

1/4 teaspoon baking powder

2/3 cup coarsely ground almonds

1/2 cup raspberry preserves

Prepare the crust: In a medium bowl, combine the flour and sugar. Using 2 knives, a pastry blender, or your fingertips, work the butter into the flour mixture until it is crumbly and resembles cornmeal. Add the cold water, a tablespoon at a time, stirring until the dough comes together into a ball.

Turn the dough out onto a lightly floured work surface and knead it once or twice. Wrap the dough in plastic wrap and chill it while you make the filling.

Preheat the oven to 375°F.

Prepare the almond filling: Using the paddle attachment of a standing electric mixer on medium speed, cream the butter, sugar, and almond paste until no lumps remain, about 2 to 3 minutes. Add the eggs, 1 at a time, mixing well before adding the next. Add the flour, baking powder, and ground almonds and mix well.

On a lightly floured work surface, roll the dough into a 13-inch round. Fit the dough carefully into a 10- or 11-inch tart pan with a removable bottom, being sure to fold the edges of the dough over twice to reinforce the sides of the tart. The doubled sides should extend slightly above the rim of the tart pan. (This allows for some shrinkage of the pastry as it bakes and will result in a strong-sided tart, capable of standing on its own and holding the filling securely.) Prick the bottom of the tart shell with a fork to prevent it from bubbling while baking.

Spread the raspberry preserves over the bottom of the tart shell. Carefully spread the almond filling over the raspberry preserves, trying not to blend the two together.

Bake the tart for 35 to 40 minutes, until the crust is lightly browned and a skewer inserted in the center comes out clean. Let the tart cool completely on a wire rack before removing it from the pan for serving on a plate.

Makes 8 to 10 servings

Pear-Almond Tart

Omit the raspberry preserves. Spread the almond filling in the chilled tart shell. Peel, halve, and core 3 ripe Bosc, Bartlett, or Anjou pears. Slice each half crosswise into ¼-inch slices. Beginning at the outer edge of the tart shell, place slices of pear overlapping each other on the almond filling, pressing them in slightly; reserve the smaller slices for the center of the tart. You should have enough slices to make 3 concentric circles of pears. Make a flower-like center with the reserved smaller pear slices. Bake the tart as directed above.

For a shiny glazed appearance, melt ½ cup apricot preserves or apple jelly in a small saucepan over medium heat until bubbly. With a pastry brush, brush the hot glaze over the entire surface of the tart. Serve warm or chilled.

Summer Vegetable Cobbler

THIS IS A HEARTY VEGETARIAN MEAL-IN-ONE-DISH. THE PESTO ADDS ZIP, BUT THE RECIPE WORKS JUST AS WELL WITHOUT IT. IF YOU DO USE PESTO, MAKE YOUR OWN, OR BUY THE REFRIGERATED—NOT JARRED—KIND FOR THE BEST RESULTS. IF YOU HAVE PLENTY OF ZUCCHINI, SUBSTITUTE 2 CUPS ZUCCHINI SLICES FOR THE CHOPPED BROCCOLI.

For the vegetable filling

2 tablespoons unsalted butter

1 medium onion, thinly sliced

2 garlic cloves, minced

1 red or green bell pepper, seeded and cut into 1/4-inch strips

2 cups chopped broccoli, blanched

1 1/2 cups sliced (1/4-inch-thick rounds) carrots, blanched

1 1/2 cups fresh or frozen corn

2 cups cold vegetable broth, homemade chicken stock, or canned chicken broth

2 tablespoons cornstarch

2 cups coarsely chopped cooked peeled potatoes

1/2 cup finely chopped fresh parsley

1/4 cup pesto

Salt and freshly ground black pepper

For the biscuit topping

2 cups all-purpose flour

2 1/2 teaspoons baking powder

1/2 teaspoon baking soda

1/4 teaspoon salt

5 tablespoons unsalted butter, cut into tablespoon-sized pieces

1 cup buttermilk

1/4 cup freshly grated Parmesan cheese

Preheat the oven to 375°F.

Prepare the vegetable filling: In a large skillet, melt the butter. Sauté the onion and garlic until the onion is translucent and softened. Add the bell pepper and sauté, stirring, for 1 to 2 minutes. Add the broccoli, carrots, and corn, then add 1½ cups of the broth and bring the liquid to a boil.

Dissolve the cornstarch in the remaining ½ cup broth and add to the skillet. Stir constantly over low heat until the sauce thickens, about 1½ minutes. Remove the pan from the heat and stir in the potatoes, parsley, and pesto. Add salt and pepper to taste. Transfer the filling to a 9 x 12-inch baking pan and chill while you make the biscuit topping.

Prepare the biscuit topping: In a large bowl, sift together the flour, baking powder, baking soda, and salt. Rub the butter into the flour mixture until it is crumbly and resembles cornmeal. Stir in the buttermilk until the dough comes together in a ball. Do not overmix.

Turn the dough out onto a lightly floured work surface and knead 2 or 3 times. Pat or gently roll the dough to a ½-inch thickness. With a 2-inch biscuit cutter, cut into rounds. Place the biscuits on top of the vegetables in the baking pan. Reroll the scraps of dough and cut biscuits in the same manner, and place on the vegetables. You will have about 15 biscuits.

Sprinkle the top of the biscuits with the Parmesan cheese. Bake the cobbler for 25 to 35 minutes, until the biscuits are browned and a skewer inserted into a biscuit comes out clean. Serve at once.

Makes 6 to 8 servings

Dilled Summer Cobbler

Omit the pesto from the vegetable filling.

Add to the dry ingredients in the biscuit topping 2 tablespoons chopped fresh parsley, 2 teaspoons chopped fresh dill, and 1 teaspoon chopped fresh thyme. Make the biscuits, assemble the cobbler, omitting the Parmesan; and bake as directed above.

Tomato and Corn Pie

LIGHTER THAN QUICHE AND CREAMIER THAN A FRITTATA, THIS CRUSTLESS SUMMER "PIE" IS BEST MADE WHEN TOMATOES AND CORN ARE AT THEIR PEAK. AFTER BAKING, THE CORN SHOULD STILL BE CRUNCHY AND THE TOMATOES DELICIOUSLY SWEET. MAKE IT A DAY AHEAD, THEN SERVE IT REHEATED OR AT ROOM TEMPERATURE. I EVEN LIKE IT CHILLED OR SERVED WITH SAUSAGES AND FRUIT FOR BREAKFAST.

3 tablespoons olive oil

1/2 onion, coarsely chopped

6 Roma or plum tomatoes, sliced a scant 1/4 inch thick

1 cup fresh or frozen corn

1/3 cup finely chopped fresh parsley

1/2 cup freshly grated Parmesan cheese

2 tablespoons balsamic vinegar (optional)

Salt and freshly ground black pepper

8 ounces cream cheese, softened

3/4 cup half-and-half

2 large eggs

1 teaspoon Dijon mustard

1/2 cup yellow cornmeal

Preheat the oven to 350°F. Generously butter a 9-inch pie plate.

In a small sauté pan or skillet, heat the olive oil over medium-high heat. Add the onion and cook for 2 to 3 minutes, until it softens and becomes translucent. Remove the pan from the heat.

In a bowl, combine the tomatoes, corn, parsley, Parmesan, vinegar, if using, and sautéed onion. Season to taste with salt and pepper.

In another bowl, using the paddle attachment of a standing electric mixer on medium speed, cream the cream cheese until light and fluffy. Gradually add the half-and-half, beating until incorporated. Add the eggs and beat until well combined. Beat in the mustard and cornmeal until combined. Using a rubber spatula, fold in the tomato and corn mixture, stirring only enough to combine. Transfer the filling to the prepared pie plate, spreading it evenly.

Bake the pie for about 25 to 30 minutes, until the edges are set and a skewer inserted near the edges comes out clean. (The center of the pie should still be slightly soft to the touch and creamy.) Let the pie cool on a wire rack for several minutes before slicing.

Makes 6 to 8 servings

Lemon Shrimp with Spicy Tomato Sauce

. . . .

THESE HOT, LEMONY SHRIMP MAKE A GREAT APPETIZER OR FIRST COURSE WHEN SERVED WITH CHUNKS OF CRUSTY BREAD TO SOAK UP THE SAUCE. ADD A CAESAR-TYPE SALAD AND A SIDE OF PLAIN PASTA, AND DINNER IS READY. FINISH WITH FRESH ESPRESSO ROMANO (WITH A TWIST OF LEMON), CHOCOLATE-DIPPED ALMOND BISCOTTI (PAGE 114), AND, FOR THOSE WHO DARE, A BOTTLE OF GRAPPA.

For the tomato sauce

1 tablespoon olive oil

3 garlic cloves, finely chopped

1 cup chopped fresh tomatoes

1 cup canned tomato purée

1/4 cup chopped scallions, including the green tops

1/2 teaspoon red pepper flakes

Juice of 2 lemons

2 to **3** tablespoons olive oil

1 1/4 pounds large shrimp, shelled, and deveined if desired

1/2 cup finely chopped fresh parsley

2 tablespoons coarsely chopped fresh basil

Prepare the tomato sauce: In a medium sauté pan or skillet, heat the olive oil over medium heat. Add the garlic and sauté for 1 minute. Add the fresh tomatoes and purée and cook for 3 to 4 minutes. Stir in the chopped scallions and red pepper flakes. Remove the pan from the heat and let the sauce cool.

Transfer the sauce to a bowl, cover, and chill until serving. Put the lemon juice in a ceramic or glass bowl; set aside.

In a large sauté pan or heavy skillet, heat 2 tablespoons olive oil until hot. Add half of the shrimp and cook over medium heat, tossing, for 1 to 2 minutes. (Do not overcook, or the shrimp will lose their delicate flavor and become tough.) The shrimp are done when they turn pink. Immediately transfer the shrimp to the bowl of lemon juice. Cook the remaining shrimp in the same manner, adding more oil to the pan if necessary. Add the second batch of cooked shrimp to the bowl and toss all the shrimp in the lemon juice. Stir in the parsley and basil.

Pour the chilled tomato sauce onto a platter. Mound the hot shrimp on the cold tomato sauce and serve at once.

Makes 4 main-course servings, 6 to 8 appetizer servings

Barbecued Spareribs

IT IS THE SAUCE THAT SEPARATES PLAIN EVERYDAY RIBS FROM *THE RIBS*. SOME RELY ON FRUIT FOR THEIR FLAVOR, OTHERS ON SPICES. BARBECUE SAUCE MADE WITH COFFEE IS UNIQUELY AMERICAN. MY VERSION IS SWEET, DARK, AND ONLY SLIGHTLY HOT, BUT BURSTING WITH FLAVOR. IT IS ALSO GREAT ON GRILLED CHICKEN OR FISH OR AS A TOPPING FOR BROILED CLAMS ON THE HALF-SHELL.

For the barbecue sauce (Makes 2 1/2 cups)

3/4 cup cider vinegar

3/4 cup balsamic vinegar

2 teaspoons whole pickling spices

2 tablespoons olive oil

1/2 cup chopped onion

2 garlic cloves, finely chopped

1 cup tomato ketchup

1/2 cup black coffee

1/4 cup unsulfured dark molasses

1/4 cup pure ground New Mexican red chile (available at some gourmet food stores) or **2** tablespoons chili powder

3 tablespoons tomato paste

2 tablespoons brown sugar

4 pounds spareribs, boneless ribs, or beef short ribs

12 ounces beer

Prepare the barbecue sauce: In a small saucepan, combine the cider vinegar, balsamic vinegar, and pickling spices and bring to a boil over high heat. Reduce the heat to medium and continue to boil the mixture, uncovered, until it is reduced to ¾ cup, about 8 to 10 minutes. Strain the vinegar through a sieve into a bowl, discard the spices, and reserve.

In a sauté pan, heat the olive oil until hot. Add the onion and garlic and sauté for 3 to 4 minutes, until the onion is translucent. Add the vinegar and all the remaining barbecue sauce ingredients, stirring until combined and smooth, and simmer the sauce over low heat for 10 to 12 minutes. Remove the pan from the heat and let cool.

Marinate the spareribs in 1 cup of the barbecue sauce, coating both sides well, covered, in the refrigerator for at least 4 hours, or overnight.

Preheat the oven to 325° F.

Place the marinated ribs on a rack or vegetable steamer in a 9 x 12-inch baking pan, and pour the beer into the pan. Cover the pan with foil and bake the ribs for 1½ hours. Remove the pan from the oven, and increase the oven temperature to 375°F. Baste or brush the ribs on both sides with additional barbecue sauce. Bake the ribs, uncovered, for 25 to 30 minutes more, basting with more sauce if desired, until the ribs are browned.

Makes 4 to 6 servings

Barbecued Grilled Vegetables

Thin the barbecue sauce with olive oil to an easy spreading consistency. Brush it on long wedges of eggplant, small zucchini, halved lengthwise, and thick slices of red onion, and grill.

Marinated Lamb Kebabs

Marinate chunks of lamb for at least 2 hours in barbecue sauce, to which 2 tablespoons fresh mint and the juice of 2 lemons have been added. Thread the lamb onto metal skewers and grill, basting frequently with the remaining sauce, until done.

Spicy Vinaigrette

Add 1 or 2 tablespoons barbecue sauce to a simple red wine vinaigrette and use as the dressing for a pasta salad made with grilled chicken, roasted bell pepper strips, sweet corn, and fresh basil leaves.

Rosemary Beef Stew
with White Wine

BEEF IS CUSTOMARILY PAIRED WITH RED WINE, BUT SOMETIMES IN COOKING ITS FLAVOR CAN BECOME TOO DARK AND PUNGENT. USING WHITE WINE ADDS PLENTY OF RICH FLAVOR, BUT THE RESULT IS NOT SO OVERPOWERING. THE LONG, SLOW COOKING TIME OF THIS STEW IS THE KEY TO ITS TENDERNESS, AND THIS IS ONE DISH THAT DOESN'T SUFFER FROM BEING REHEATED. IN FACT, IT'S BETTER THE SECOND DAY.

7 slices bacon, diced

2 1/2 pounds beef rump roast, cut into 1 1/2-inch cubes

2 to **3** tablespoons olive oil

1 onion, thinly sliced

3 garlic cloves, finely chopped

1 tablespoon brown sugar

3 tablespoons unsalted butter

1/4 cup all-purpose flour

1 1/2 cups dry white wine

2 cups homemade beef stock or canned beef broth

1 tablespoon balsamic vinegar

1 tablespoon tomato paste

2 bay leaves

2 teaspoons chopped fresh rosemary or **1** teaspoon dried rosemary

Salt and freshly ground black pepper to taste

1 pound baby carrots

12 to **15** small new potatoes or **3** cups peeled and chopped medium-size (1 1/2-inch) potatoes

Preheat the oven to 325°F.

In a large skillet, cook the bacon over medium heat until it is browned and no fat remains. With a slotted spoon, remove the bacon to paper towels to drain. Reserve the pan drippings.

Pat the beef cubes dry with paper towels (or they will not brown). Add the olive oil to the drippings in the skillet and heat over medium-high heat. Cook the beef in batches until it is browned on all sides. Transfer the beef to a large casserole.

Reduce the heat under the skillet to medium, and add the onion and garlic, and cook until the onion is softened and translucent. Add the sugar and cook, stirring, a few minutes more. Transfer to the casserole.

Melt the butter in the skillet over medium-low heat. Add the flour, stirring to form a paste, and cook until it browns slightly. Gradually add the wine, stock, and vinegar, stirring constantly. Add the tomato

Roasted Eggplant and
Tomato Soup
(PAGE 100)

Rosemary Beef
Stew with White Wine

Salad of
Mixed Wild Greens

Sourdough Rolls

Mascarpone Cheesecake
(PAGE 134)

Cardamon and Orange
Coffee
(PAGE 77)

Barbecued Spareribs
(PAGE 128)

Cornmeal Muffins
(PAGE 88)

Butter Lettuce and
Tomato Salad
with Creamy Dill
Dressing

Corn on the Cob

Chocolate-Mint
Pots de Crème
(PAGE 138)

Café Midnight
(PAGE 77)

paste and bring the liquid to a boil. Reduce the heat to low, add the bay leaves and rosemary, and simmer for 5 minutes. Add salt and pepper to taste. Pour the sauce over the meat, stir in the reserved cooked bacon, and cover the casserole. Bake for 1½ hours.

Add the carrots and potatoes to the stew. Cover and bake for 45 minutes to 1 hour more, until the vegetables are cooked through but still firm.

Makes 4 to 6 servings

Chili con Carne

· ·

CHILI CON CARNE, LIKE COFFEE BEANS, HAS MANY IDENTITIES. THIS ONE IS MIDWESTERN IN STYLE, MEANING IT IS MADE NOT WITH PIECES OF BEEF BUT WITH GROUND BEEF. IT COOKS UP SOUTHWEST-STYLE, THOUGH, BECAUSE OF THE BEER AND PURE GROUND NEW MEXICAN RED CHILE. YOU CAN ALSO MAKE IT WITH GROUND TURKEY OR CUBED BEEF STEW MEAT. HOT CORNMEAL MUFFINS (PAGE 88) ARE THE PERFECT ACCOMPANIMENT.

3 tablespoons olive oil

1 1/2 pounds ground beef (ground coarse for chili)

1 onion, coarsely chopped

1 green bell pepper, seeded and coarsely chopped

1 stalk celery, chopped

4 garlic cloves, coarsely chopped

1 cup beer

1/2 cup black coffee

2 cups canned tomatoes, diced, with their juice

Two 15-ounce cans red beans or pinto beans, drained and rinsed

1/3 cup mild pure ground New Mexican red chile (available at some gourmet food stores) or **2** tablespoons plus **2** teaspoons chili powder

1 teaspoon ground cumin

1 teaspoon dried oregano

Salt and freshly ground black pepper

Chopped cilantro, for garnish

In a large heavy-bottomed saucepan, heat the olive oil until hot. Add the ground beef, onion, green pepper, celery, and garlic and cook over medium-high heat, stirring, for 3 to 5 minutes, until the beef is lightly browned and the vegetables have softened. Add the beer and coffee and cook, stirring frequently, for 2 to 3 minutes. Add the tomatoes and their juice, the beans, ground chile, cumin, and oregano. Bring the mixture to a boil, reduce the heat to low, and cook, partially covered, for 25 to 35 minutes, stirring occasionally. Season to taste with salt and pepper.

Serve in bowls and garnish with chopped cilantro.

Makes 6 servings

Queen Anne Cherry Strudel

· ·

YOU CAN MAKE A SIMPLE BUT VERY GOOD SAUCE FOR THIS STRUDEL USING THE SYRUP FROM THE CHERRIES. IN A SMALL SAUCEPAN, COOK THE SYRUP OVER MEDIUM HEAT, SIMMERING IT GENTLY UNTIL IT IS REDUCED TO THE CONSISTENCY OF A THIN PURÉE. ADD A SQUEEZE OF FRESH LEMON JUICE AND A DASH OF RUM, AND SERVE THE SAUCE WARM ON THE STILL-WARM STRUDEL.

Two 16-ounce cans Queen Anne cherries in syrup, drained

1/4 cup firmly packed light brown sugar

1 teaspoon vanilla extract

1/3 cup sour cream

1 tablespoon plus 2 teaspoons cornstarch

1/2 teaspoon freshly grated nutmeg

6 sheets phyllo dough

5 tablespoons unsalted butter, melted

1 cup fresh bread crumbs

Confectioners' sugar, for dusting

Preheat the oven to 375°F. Lightly grease a baking sheet.

In a bowl, combine the cherries, brown sugar, vanilla extract, sour cream, cornstarch, and nutmeg; set aside.

On a work surface, brush the tops of 3 sheets of the phyllo dough with some of the melted butter and stack them on top of one another. Sprinkle the top sheet with ½ cup of the bread crumbs. Brush the remaining 3 sheets of phyllo lightly with some of the butter, stack them on top of the first sheets, and sprinkle the top sheet with the remaining ½ cup bread crumbs.

Arrange the stack of phyllo sheets on the work surface so that a long edge faces you. Leaving a 1-inch border along the longer edge, spread the filling in a strip down the length of the stack, leaving a 1-inch border at either end. Starting with the edge in front of you, fold the phyllo over the filling, then roll up the phyllo, enclosing the filling. Turn the strudel seam side down and tuck the open ends under the roll to seal them.

With your hands, transfer the strudel carefully, still seam side down, to the prepared baking sheet. Brush the dough with the remaining butter. Bake the strudel for 35 to 40 minutes, until the dough is crisp and lightly browned. Sprinkle with confectioners' sugar, slice it, and serve.

Makes 6 to 8 servings

Mascarpone Cheesecake

· ·

MASCARPONE IS SOMETIMES CALLED ITALIAN CREAM CHEESE, BUT IT BEARS ALMOST NO RESEMBLANCE TO WHAT AMERICANS HAVE COME TO KNOW AS CREAM CHEESE. MASCARPONE IS CREAMIER AND RICHER AND HAS AN INCREDIBLE BUTTERY TASTE, PERFECT FOR CHEESECAKE. THIS IS A DESSERT FOR A SPECIAL OCCASION.

For the crust

2 cups cookie crumbs, such as vanilla sugar wafer or graham cracker crumbs

1/4 cup sugar

5 tablespoons unsalted butter, melted

For the filling

1 1/2 pounds cream cheese, at room temperature

1 1/4 cups sugar

Two 200-gram containers of mascarpone (available at specialty or gourmet food markets)

4 large eggs

3 large egg yolks

1/2 cup golden raisins (optional)

Grated zest of 1 lemon

Grated zest of 1 orange

Preheat the oven to 400°F.

Prepare the crust: In a bowl, combine the cookie crumbs and sugar with the butter. Press the mixture over the bottom of a 10-inch springform pan; set aside.

Prepare the filling: Using the paddle attachment of a standing electric mixer on medium speed, beat the cream cheese until no lumps remain. Add the sugar and beat until light and creamy. Add the mascarpone and continue to beat until smooth. Add the eggs and egg yolks and beat until well combined. Add the raisins, if using, and lemon and orange zests and stir until thoroughly combined. Pour the filling into the prepared pan.

Place the cheesecake in the oven and reduce the oven temperature to 300°F. Bake the cheesecake for 1 hour. Turn the oven off, but let the cheesecake remain in the oven until cooled and set, at least 1½ hours, or as long as overnight.

Cover the cheesecake with plastic wrap and chill thoroughly for easy slicing. Serve as is or with unsweetened whipped cream.

Makes 10 to 12 servings

Hazelnut Mascarpone Cheesecake

Omit the raisins and lemon and orange zests, and add ¾ cup toasted ground hazelnuts and 1 teaspoon almond extract to the filling mixture. Bake the cheesecake as directed above.

Espresso Chocolate Mascarpone Cheesecake

Omit the raisins and lemon and orange zests, and add 2 ounces grated bittersweet or semisweet chocolate and 1 tablespoon instant coffee dissolved in 2 tablespoons hot espresso or coffee to the filling mixture. Bake the cheesecake as directed above.

Lemon Mascarpone Cheesecake with Raspberries

Omit the raisins and orange zest, and add the zest of 1 additional lemon plus the juice of 2 lemons to the filling mixture. Just before turning the batter into the prepared pan, gently stir in ½ pint fresh raspberries. Bake the cheesecake as directed above.

Crème Brûlée

· ·

THERE IS NOTHING LOW-FAT ABOUT CRÈME BRÛLÉE, BUT THERE IS ALSO NOTHING LIKE ITS SIMPLE CREAMINESS TOPPED WITH CARAMEL CRUNCH. LIGHTER VERSIONS DO EXIST, BUT THIS ONE IS THE REAL THING. DON'T OVERBAKE, OR THE CUSTARDS WILL CURDLE. THEY WILL STILL TASTE DELICIOUS, BUT THE SMOOTH SATINY TEXTURE, WHICH IS WHAT CRÈME BRÛLÉE IS ALL ABOUT, WILL BE SPOILED.

9 large egg yolks

1/3 cup sugar, plus additional sugar for caramelizing

1 cup half-and-half

3 cups heavy cream

1 vanilla bean, split lengthwise

Preheat the oven to 325°F.

In a medium-size bowl, whisk together the egg yolks and ⅓ cup sugar.

In a medium-size saucepan, combine the half-and-half and heavy cream. Add the vanilla bean. Heat the mixture over medium heat until scalded (a skin will form on top). Pour one third of the scalded cream over the egg mixture, whisking to combine. Then pour the yolk-cream mixture into the saucepan and whisk to combine with the remaining cream. Strain the custard through a medium-mesh strainer into a bowl or pitcher. Discard the vanilla bean.

Divide the custard among six 6-ounce custard cups and place the filled cups in a 9 x 12-inch baking pan. Fill the baking pan with enough hot water to reach halfway up the sides of the cups. Bake for about 1 hour, or until the surface of the custards appears set around the edges but the centers are still wobbly. Remove the custard cups from the water bath and let cool completely on a wire rack.

Just before serving, preheat the broiler. Sprinkle a scant tablespoon of sugar evenly over the surface of each custard. Place the custard cups on a baking sheet and place under the broiler on the rack closest to the source of heat. In a matter of seconds, the sugar will begin to melt and caramelize to a golden brown. Remove from the broiler immediately—sugar burns very quickly—and serve.

Makes 6 servings

. . . .

Ginger Crème Brûlée

Omit the vanilla bean and add 2 tablespoons grated fresh ginger to the cream mixture before scalding it. Strain the custard to remove the ginger, bake, and caramelize as directed above.

Cappuccino Crème Brûlée

Add 2 tablespoons instant coffee dissolved in 2 tablespoons hot espresso or coffee with ¼ teaspoon cinnamon added to the egg yolk and sugar mixture. Bake and caramelize as directed above.

Raspberry Crème Brûlée

Add 6 fresh or frozen unsweetened raspberries to each custard cup before baking. Bake and caramelize as directed above.

Grand Marnier Crème Brûlée

Omit the vanilla bean and add 3 tablespoons grated orange zest to the cream mixture before scalding it. Strain the custard into a bowl and discard the orange zest. Stir 3 tablespoons Grand Marnier into the custard before dividing it among the ramekins. Bake and caramelize as directed above.

Chocolate-Mint Pots de Crème

TRADITIONALLY, POTS DE CRÈME ARE BAKED IN TINY COVERED POTS; IF YOU ARE LUCKY ENOUGH TO HAVE A SET OF THESE DELICATE CERAMIC DISHES, USE THEM. BUT THE RICH CREAMY TASTE OF THIS DESSERT IS JUST AS WONDERFUL IF YOU USE CUSTARD CUPS INSTEAD. GARNISH EACH WITH A FRESH MINT LEAF OR A SLIVER OF ORANGE PEEL DIPPED IN EGG WHITE AND ROLLED IN SUGAR AND SAVOR THEM STRAIGHT UP WITH ESPRESSO.

6 large egg yolks

2 tablespoons white *crème de menthe*

2 cups half-and-half

2/3 cup heavy cream

8 ounces semisweet chocolate, melted

Preheat the oven to 325°F.

Place the egg yolks and *crème de menthe* in a blender. In a medium-size saucepan, combine the half-and-half and heavy cream and bring to a boil. Use a rubber spatula to scrape the melted chocolate into the blender and pour the boiling cream mixture on top. Cover and turn the blender on to medium speed. Blend for 15 to 20 seconds until all the ingredients are well combined.

Divide the mixture among six 6-ounce ramekins or custard cups. Place the ramekins in a 9 x 12-inch baking pan, fill the pan with hot water to come halfway up the sides of the ramekins, and carefully place the pan in the oven. Bake about 40 minutes, or until the custard is set.

Remove the ramekins from the water bath and let them cool on a rack. Then chill at least 2 to 3 hours before serving.

Makes 6 servings

Chocolate Zabaglione

I HAVE REDUCED THE AMOUNT OF MARSALA THAT IS CUSTOMARILY USED IN THIS FAMOUS FROTHY ITALIAN DESSERT SO THAT IT IS NEITHER TOO INTENSE NOR TOO SWEET. BECAUSE OF THE MELTED CHOCOLATE AND WHIPPED CREAM, THIS VERSION RESEMBLES A SILKEN CHOCOLATE MOUSSE. LIKE CLASSIC ZABAGLIONE, IT IS VERY GOOD SERVED WITH FRESH STRAWBERRIES OR RASPBERRIES.

5 large egg yolks

1/3 cup sugar

1/3 cup Marsala

4 ounces semisweet chocolate, melted and cooled

1 tablespoon dark rum or amaretto

1 cup chilled heavy cream whipped just until stiff

Additional heavy cream, for serving (optional)

In a large metal bowl set over a half-filled pan of simmering water, whip the egg yolks with a balloon whisk until slightly thickened and light in color. Add the sugar, 1 tablespoon at a time, continuing to whip rapidly with the whisk until the mixture thickens, turns pale in color, and reaches the consistency of a thin mayonnaise, about 5 to 7 minutes in all.

Add the Marsala, a tablespoon at a time, continuing to whip vigorously and constantly, until the mixture again thickens and becomes light, about 2 to 3 minutes.

Remove the bowl from the pan and whisk the mixture for 1 or 2 minutes more. Stir in the melted chocolate and rum. If the bowl is still warm to the touch, refrigerate the mixture until the bowl is cool and the custard has cooled to room temperature. Gently fold the whipped cream into the chilled custard. Spoon the zabaglione into parfait glasses and garnish with additional whipped cream, if desired.

Makes 4 to 6 servings

Espresso Granita

THIS SIMPLE DESSERT IS TRULY REFRESHING, AND WITH ITS ICY GRANULAR TEXTURE IT IS A COMPLETE DEPARTURE FROM OTHER FROZEN DESSERTS LIKE ICE CREAM OR EVEN SORBET. IN ITALY, WHERE GRANITA ORIGINATED, SCOOPS ARE OFTEN TOPPED WITH HEAVY CREAM OR CROWNED WITH A BILLOW OF VERY SOFTLY WHIPPED CREAM.

1 cup water

1/2 cup sugar

3 cups fresh-brewed espresso

In a small saucepan, combine the water and sugar and bring to a boil over high heat. Reduce the heat to medium and cook for 4 to 5 minutes. Stir in the espresso. Pour the mixture into a 9 x 13-inch baking pan and place the pan in the freezer until the ice is completely frozen, at least 4 hours.

Using the tines of a fork, scrape the ice into shavings; spoon the shavings at once into chilled dessert glasses and serve immediately.

Makes 6 small servings

Rich Dark Gingerbread

THIS IS DELICIOUS BY ITSELF, ALTHOUGH THE SHARP TASTES OF GRATED FRESH GINGER, COFFEE, AND BLACKSTRAP MOLASSES PAIR WELL WITH ICE CREAM OR ANY SWEETENED CREAM OR FRUIT. A SMALL PIECE OF THIS SERVED WARM WITH WHIPPED CREAM AND SAUTÉED SLICED PEARS MAKES AN EXCELLENT END TO ANY MEAL.

2 cups all-purpose flour

1 teaspoon baking powder

1/2 teaspoon baking soda

1/2 teaspoon cinnamon

1/4 teaspoon cloves

1/2 cup (1 stick) unsalted butter, at room temperature

1/3 cup firmly packed dark brown sugar

2 large eggs

2/3 cup blackstrap molasses or other dark, full-flavored molasses

1/2 cup sour cream

2 teaspoons instant coffee dissolved in 1/4 cup hot coffee

2 tablespoons grated fresh ginger

Preheat the oven to 350°F. Grease and flour a 9-inch springform pan or 9-inch square baking pan.

Sift together the flour, baking powder, baking soda, cinnamon, and cloves onto a sheet of waxed paper; set aside.

Using the paddle attachment of a standing electric mixer on medium speed, cream the butter and brown sugar until light and fluffy. Add the eggs, one at a time, mixing until incorporated before adding the next. Stir in the molasses until completely blended. Add the sour cream, coffee, and ginger and blend until well combined. Add the dry ingredients and beat until the batter is smooth.

Pour the batter into the prepared pan. Bake it for 25 to 35 minutes, or until the edges of the gingerbread pull away from the sides of the pan and the center springs back when lightly touched with a fingertip. Let the gingerbread cool slightly on a wire rack before cutting it into wedges or into 2¼-inch squares. Serve warm or at room temperature.

Makes twelve 2 1/4 -inch squares

Bittersweet Chocolate Sauce

I'VE NEVER HAD TO TALK ANYONE INTO HAVING CHOCOLATE SAUCE! HOWEVER, SHOULD A LITTLE CONVINCING BE NECESSARY, THIS ONE IS ESPECIALLY GOOD ON ICE CREAM, CHEESECAKE, OR BROWNIES, OR AS A DESSERT FONDUE: USE CHUNKS OF FRESH FRUIT OR BERRIES FOR DIPPING. THE COFFEE OR COFFEE LIQUEUR IN THE SAUCE CAN BE REPLACED WITH A LITTLE COGNAC, AMARETTO, GRAND MARNIER, OR RUM.

10 ounces good-quality bittersweet chocolate, such as Lindt, Toblerone, Callebaut, or Ghirardelli, coarsely chopped

1/2 cup half-and-half

Zest of 1 orange, removed in strips with a peeler

1/4 cup extra-strong coffee or coffee liqueur, such as Kahlúa

Place the chopped chocolate in a heat-proof metal or glass bowl.

In a saucepan, combine the half-and-half and orange zest and bring to a boil. Strain the mixture through a sieve into a heat-proof measuring cup and discard the orange zest. Pour the hot half-and-half over the chopped chocolate and stir until smooth. Stir in the coffee.

Use the sauce at once or let it cool slightly, then transfer it to a jar. Let the sauce cool in the jar, cover it, and refrigerate until ready to use. The sauce will harden when chilled; to serve, heat the sauce in a small saucepan over low heat, stirring often, until melted.

Makes 1 1/2 cups

Recipe Index

Acknowledgments

SMALLWOOD AND STEWART WISH TO THANK

PETER LONGO OF PORTO RICO IMPORTING COMPANY

OF NEW YORK AND DOUGLAS CARPENTER

FOR THEIR INVALUABLE ASSISTANCE.

Photography Credits

Maria Ferrari: ENDPAPERS, 18, 38, 50, 68. Doug Plummer: 1. Marcus Pietrek/Impact: 2, 73.
William Stites: 6, 44, 45, 46, 49, 52, 70. Gregory Clark: 8, 58, 66. Jean-Loup Charmet: 11, 54. E.T. Archive: 12.
Culver Pictures, Inc.: 14, 144. Studio Mike/Leo de Wys Inc.: 17, 24. Sam Abell/Woodfin Camp:
20, 55, 56, 57. Christopher Cormack/Impact: 23. Dave Bartruff/Artistry International: 26. John Cole/Impact: 27.
J. Messerschmidt/Leo de Wys Inc.: 28. Robert Holmes: 30, 32, 35, 42, 43, 64. Robert Opie: 37, 59, 60.
Greene/Archive: 40. Walt Anderson: 53. © John Margolies/Esto: 67